A Biblical Way of Praying the Mass

Other books by Fr. Timothy M. Gallagher, O.M.V.
from EWTN Publishing and Sophia Institute Press:

A Layman's Guide to the Liturgy of the Hours
How the Prayers of the Church Can Change Your Life

Overcoming Spiritual Discouragement
The Wisdom and Spiritual Power of Venerable Bruno Lanteri

Discernment of Spirits in Marriage
Ignatian Wisdom for Husbands and Wives

Timothy M. Gallagher, O.M.V.

A Biblical Way of Praying the Mass

The Eucharistic Wisdom of Venerable Bruno Lanteri

EWTN PUBLISHING, INC.
Irondale, Alabama

Imprimi potest: Fr. James A. Walther, O.M.V.,
Provincial of the Province of St. Ignatius
October 27, 2020

EWTN Publishing, Inc.
5817 Old Leeds Road, Irondale, AL 35210

Distributed by Sophia Institute Press, Box 5284, Manchester, NH 03108.

Library of Congress Cataloging-in-Publication Data

Names: Gallagher, Timothy M., author.
Title: A biblical way of praying the mass : the eucharistic wisdom of
  Venerable Bruno Lanteri / Timothy M. Gallagher, OMV.
Description: Irondale, Alabama : EWTN Publishing, Inc., [2020] | Includes
  bibliographical references. | Summary: "Using a method by Venerable
  Bruno Lanteri, the author explains how to adopt the dispositions of
  various biblical figures and saints in order to pray the Mass more
  fruitfully"— Provided by publisher.
Identifiers: LCCN 2020039442 | ISBN 9781682782279 (paperback) | ISBN
  9781682782286 (ebook)
Subjects: LCSH: Lord's Supper. | Prayer—Catholic Church. | Lanteri, Pio
  Brunone, 1759-1830.
Classification: LCC BX2230.3 .G35 2020 | DDC 264/.36—dc23
LC record available at https://lccn.loc.gov/2020039442

From the Decree of Saint Paul VI Declaring the Heroicity of the Virtues of Venerable Bruno Lanteri:

His Holiness, Paul VI, having prayed earnestly, in conclusion, on this day, after celebrating Mass with great fervor, called the Most Reverend Cardinals Arcadio Maria Larraona, Prefect of the Sacred Congregation of Rites; Benedetto Aloisi Masella, Relator of the Cause; and me with them, as Secretary, and solemnly decreed that "the Servant of God, Pio Brunone Lanteri, priest and founder of the Congregation of the Oblates of the Virgin Mary, practiced the theological virtues of faith, hope, and charity toward God and neighbor, as also the cardinal virtues of prudence, justice, temperance, and fortitude, with their associated virtues, to a heroic degree."

Rome, 23 November 1965

Arcadio Card. M. Larraona,
Prefect of the Sacred Congregation of Rites

Ferdinando Antonelli, O.F.M., Secretary

Venerable Bruno Lanteri (1759–1830)

Contents

Acknowledgments

I am deeply grateful to all who have helped me in the writing and publication of this book: to those who read the manuscript and offered invaluable advice: Elizabeth Valeri, Kate Sell, Joe Patrnchak, James Gallagher, and Susan Mire; to Charlie McKinney of Sophia Institute Press for his guidance in the process of publication; to Devin Jones and all at EWTN for their assistance and support for this book; to Anna Maria Mendell for her capable help with the images included in the book; and in particular to Nora Malone for her competent and dedicated editing in preparing the book for publication. To all, my sincere thanks.

A Biblical Way of Praying the Mass

Introduction

Who of us does not cherish the Mass — and also desire to pray it more deeply? We assist at Mass on Sundays and many of us on weekdays as well. We love the Mass. We share the Church's faith in the Mass. We know it to be, as the Second Vatican Council affirms, the "source and summit of the Christian life."[1] And yet ... more than we wish, when we are at Mass, it seems to pass us by. The Introductory Rites conclude almost before we know it. After the readings, we might struggle to recall what they were about. The Eucharistic Prayer with the Consecration is over in a moment. We receive Jesus in Communion and are grateful ... but we also wish we lived this gift more deeply. We return to our activity after Mass ... and would want the Mass to touch our day more fully.

Forty-five years ago, I learned of a way to pray the Mass that has blessed me ever since. I found it in the writings of Venerable Bruno Lanteri (1759–1830). He composed this text for himself as a seminarian and practiced it throughout his life. He then gave it to his priests and, through them, to us all.

Venerable Bruno lived in northern Italy in the turbulent times before, during, and after the French Revolution. He experienced

---

[1] Second Vatican Council, Dogmatic Constitution on the Church *Lumen Gentium* (November 21, 1964), no. 11.

war, political subjection, persecution, and unending struggles of health. Through it all, he remained solidly rooted in Christ and a sure source of strength for the many people who sought his spiritual aid.[2]

For him, at the heart of everything lay the Eucharist. Here he encountered Christ; here he found love, courage, strength, and hope.

In order truly to *pray* the Mass, he chose various biblical figures whose sentiments he wished to share at corresponding parts of the Mass. This helped him pray the Mass from the *heart*. The fruitfulness of this practice revealed itself in his life.

Over the years, I have come to love this approach. Those with whom I share it esteem it as well. For most, this way of praying the Mass is new; for all, it is fresh, warm, and alive. It responds in a practical way to the need described above. It is uncomplicated. It leads to the heart of the Mass. It transforms presence at Mass into prayer. It excludes no one.

The goal of this book is to offer this way of praying the Mass to all.

Each chapter describes how the biblical person chosen relates to the part of the Mass in question. The chapter then proposes exercises for appropriating the disposition described. The book may simply be read, but I believe it will bear more fruit if the reader, even briefly, prays the exercises provided. The corresponding images supplied in the color section of this book, when viewed in

---

[2] For a biography and general information regarding the life and teaching of Venerable Bruno Lanteri, see the Resources section at the conclusion of this book. For a brief description of Venerable Bruno's approach to praying the Mass, see Timothy Gallagher, O.M.V., *Overcoming Spiritual Discouragement: The Wisdom and Spiritual Power of Venerable Bruno Lanteri* (Irondale, AL: EWTN Publishing, 2019), 38–45.

conjunction with the exercises, will further strengthen this prayer. If the chapters are read and prayed in this way, Venerable Bruno's approach will emerge more readily during Mass. An occasional return to these exercises may help keep the approach fresh and alive.

To render this way of praying the Mass more accessible, I have included a summary of the method at the end of the book. This summary may be retained in the book or detached and used for prayer when at Mass.

May Venerable Bruno's invitation to *pray* the Mass lead us ever more deeply into the Mass's inexhaustible richness.

Venerable Bruno's Text

When I enter the church, I will imagine that I see Simeon, who went in the Spirit to the Temple for the presentation and circumcision of Jesus, or I will imagine seeing some other fervent saint.

In the Mass, at the Penitential Rite, I will seek the sentiments and the heart of the tax collector.

At the Gloria, those of the Angels.

At the Prayers, those of an ambassador sent by the Church.

At the Readings and Gospel, those of a disciple.

At the Profession of Faith, those of the martyrs.

At the Preparation of the Gifts, those of Melchizedek.

At the Preface, those of the Heavenly Court.

At the Consecration, those of Christ.

At the Our Father, those of one who asks for what he needs.

At the Lamb of God, those of one who is guilty and in need of forgiveness.

At Communion, those of one in love.

At the words "Go forth, the Mass is ended," those of an apostle.

I will go forth from the altar as if breathing fire.

1

A Personal Word

From my earliest recollection, the Mass was always present. My dad's Irish father raised him in this practice. His Protestant mother added a reverence for and familiarity with the Bible that he passed on to us. My mother was a convert and deeply attached to the Catholic faith.

We went to Mass every Sunday. Our parish, Most Holy Rosary, was a short drive away, and we participated regularly in its life. I will be forever grateful to Father James Woulfe, our pastor for twenty-seven years and the face of the priesthood for me through those years. A second priest, Father Donald Van Amburgh, principal of our Catholic high school, helped with Sunday Masses. We looked forward to his presence and his preaching.

Once age permitted, my brothers and I served Mass in the parish. This brought us close to the Mass and habituated us to its ceremonies and the sacred vessels. My father attended daily Mass in the morning on his way to work. We often accompanied him and served the Mass. Once we children were older, my mother went to evening Mass during the week, and at times we would attend Mass with her. During Lent, the sisters who taught us at school brought us to church for daily Mass. Through these various channels, the Mass was for us, in practice, the "source and summit" of our Catholic life, as Vatican II described it in these same years.[3] Everything in our faith flowed from the Mass as its center.

My siblings and I learned about the Mass from catechism and at home. I remember in particular when my mother read Monsignor Ronald Knox's *The Mass in Slow Motion* to us. Its blend of warm humor and solid content made it easy to absorb.

When I entered the seminary, this familiarity with the Mass deepened. We had classes on the sacraments and in-house training for the ministries of lector and acolyte, preparatory to ordination. Once installed as an acolyte, I helped in the distribution of Communion, a major new step. During these years, I learned of and read Saint Leonard of Port Maurice's *The Hidden Treasure*. It has stayed in my memory as a devotional aid to praying the Mass.

I was ordained a deacon in September of 1978. A month later, Saint John Paul II was elected pope. Because we were in Rome, my companions and I served on various occasions as deacons for the new pope. It was a great blessing.

I assisted Pope John Paul II as deacon three times, twice in Saint Peter's and once in the Jesuit church in Rome, the Gesù. Each time, I did the same: as much as diaconal functions permitted, I simply watched him pray. The image of this man absorbed in prayer, even under television cameras and surrounded by thousands of people, has always remained with me.

I still smile at one memory. From time to time, Saint John Paul II would look up from his prayer with a gaze of penetrating awareness. You felt that he perceived all that surrounded him. Whenever the pope looked up, I would immediately drop my eyes. When he

---

[3] Second Vatican Council, Dogmatic Constitution on the Church *Lumen Gentium* (November 21, 1964), no. 11.

returned to his prayer, I would resume watching him. Saint John Paul II showed me what it means to understand the richness of the Mass and to pray it from the heart.

During my seminary years, like many others, I listened to Venerable Fulton Sheen's talks to priests. From them, I assimilated his repeated invitation to make a daily Holy Hour before the Blessed Sacrament. When I learned that Venerable Bruno Lanteri, the founder of my community, also called us to a daily hour of meditation, the double invitation spoke to my heart, and I wanted to respond. For a time, I made this meditation in the quiet of my room. Before long, however, I chose to do it before the Blessed Sacrament.

Over the years, I have come to appreciate deeply the richness of such prayer. The presence of Jesus in the Eucharist blesses prayer in a unique way. You may battle with distractions and tiredness. You may struggle to stay the whole time and really to pray. But you know that you are not alone. You sense the Real Presence, and it changes the day that follows.

A memory of my mother surfaces as I write this. After priestly ordination, when I would return home to visit, I would go to our parish for my meditation. My mother, if she was free, would accompany me. Her prayer had grown over the years, and I can still see her, a few feet away, quietly absorbed in prayer, with little movement, simply centered on the Lord. She showed me what can happen when a person prays faithfully through the years—how prayer simplifies, captivates, transforms, and gives strength for the responsibilities a person carries.

Once ordained, I was assigned as assistant to our novice master. Among other tasks, he asked me to speak to the novices on the role of Scripture in the spiritual life. I was ordained only a few months, and everything was new. To prepare the talks—what do you say to a group of twenty novices?—much reading and reflection was necessary. We had studied Scripture in the seminary, but this was different: this time I was to be the teacher. The topic was not, as then, the history or interpretation of Scripture; I was to speak on the place of God's Word in our spiritual lives.

I read the Church Fathers on the Bible, the relevant Church documents, and various other authors. From this emerged ten talks that I gave to the novices. Whatever they may have learned, my reading helped me to understand Scripture in a new way. The Church Fathers' love for the Bible and their perception of it as a love letter from God to each of us instilled in me a new reverence for the Bible. More deeply than before, I grasped and, above all, *felt* its uniqueness and power.

For the first time, too, I appreciated the richness of the Liturgy of the Word, that part of the Mass in which the readings, psalm, and Gospel are proclaimed. One key truth came alive for me: when these readings are proclaimed at Mass, *Jesus is present* in the midst of his people, *speaking his word to them.* In the Liturgy of the Word, we share the experience of those who heard Jesus speak on the mountainside, by the lake, and in the Temple. We are there at his feet as he speaks to us. This understanding led to a new esteem for the Liturgy of the Word.

In my second year of priesthood, I was assigned to a small parish near Milan, in northern Italy. A priest was needed, and the superiors wanted me to experience parish life. I spent a year there, a blessed experience for which I remain grateful.

I learned what it means to walk with people in a parish, to share their lives, and to serve as their priest. My community also served the neighboring parish, and life was busy. On some days, I celebrated five Masses. When later I was sent to our seminary residence in Boston, I was given charge of our Hispanic community. I served in this position for five years. I loved it and came to know the people deeply. Homilies in Spanish required effort, but the spiritual and human rewards of pastoral life with the people were wonderful. Sunday Mass was the center of this ministry, and we prepared it well with music, Eucharistic ministers, readers, and servers.

After my years as provincial of our Oblate United States province, I chose to spend my sabbatical in a parish. I resided there for a year and a half and, when my retreat work resumed, continued to help on weekends when I could. Again, Mass was the center—Sunday and daily Mass while I lived there, and Sunday Mass after. Here again, I experienced the power of Mass with a parish: the warm greetings when you arrive, the preparations for the Mass, the celebration of Mass itself, and the conversations with people after.

For years now, I have lived an itinerant life, traveling for retreats and conferences. I love the opportunity to speak of spiritual things in these settings. One experience regarding travel and the Mass often repeats.

The trip to the airport usually requires an early start. Because I will have no opportunity later, I celebrate a private Mass before I leave. This involves rising earlier on an already early morning, but that Mass makes a great difference in the day. I finish the Mass, gather my things, and head to the airport feeling nourished and ready for the travel and the event to come. As it does in all circumstances, the Mass blesses these days of travel.

When a new papal encyclical or apostolic letter appears, I always try to read it. This has proved beneficial as regards the Mass. Saint John Paul II spoke of how consideration of the Eucharist "leads us to profound amazement and gratitude" and of his desire to "rekindle this Eucharistic 'amazement.'"[4] His words resonated because I desired a deeper appreciation of the Mass and wished to pray it increasingly from the heart.

On various occasions, Benedict XVI cited the forty-nine Christians of the fourth century who defied the emperor's prohibition to celebrate Mass. One Sunday, while gathered at Mass, they were discovered. They were arrested and brought before the Roman proconsul. When asked why they had defied the emperor's orders, well knowing that death would be the penalty, one replied, "*Sine dominico non possumus*," that is, "Without Sunday Mass we cannot live."[5] Pope Francis has continued this emphasis on the Mass, reminding us that "the Mass is prayer; rather, it is prayer par excellence, the loftiest, the most sublime, and at the same time the most 'concrete.'"[6]

The words of Vatican II already cited, that the Eucharist is "the source and summit" of the Christian life, have always remained with me. The *source*: everything in our lives as Christians flows from the Eucharist; the *summit*: all else in our lives as Christians is directed toward the Eucharist. When I compare my own experience of the Mass with this teaching, a desire awakens, a need, a search for a way to live the Mass with this depth, that is, truly to pray the Mass.

This is where Venerable Bruno's text enters.

When I joined the Oblates of the Virgin Mary, I came to know its founder, the Venerable Bruno Lanteri. He drew me from the start, and this attraction has never waned. I read all that I could

4   Pope Saint John Paul II, Encyclical Letter *Ecclesia de Eucharistia* April 17, 2003), nos. 5, 6.
5   Pope Benedict XVI, Post-Synodal Apostolic Exhortation *Sacramentum Caritatis* (February 22, 2007), no. 95
6   Pope Francis, General Audience, November 15, 2017.

find about him, dedicated a part of my studies to him, wrote my graduate theses about him, visited the places of his life, and later taught his spirituality to the seminarians of our order. I explored his writings in the archives and wrote books about his life and spiritual teaching.

From seminary days, his approach to the Mass caught my attention in a lasting way. In it, Venerable Bruno shaped a personal way to pray the Mass—not simply to perform the ceremonies well, but truly to *pray it from the heart.*

I was then and remain now struck by the simplicity and practicality of this text. Venerable Bruno chooses a biblical figure for each part of the Mass: Simeon as we enter the church, the tax collector (Luke 18:9–14) as we pray the penitential rite, the angels on Christmas night as we pray the Gloria, the disciples listening to Jesus as the readings are proclaimed, and in like fashion for the entire Mass. Delving into the heart of that person, he finds the ideal sentiments to live the corresponding part of the Mass—that is, *to pray it.* His approach is simple and profound.

Through the years of my priesthood, this text has always been present. At times, I live it more deeply, at times less, but it is always there. I have placed it on the wall near the altar where I often celebrate Mass, and I see it nearly every day.

One year, as Lent was beginning, I shared on Facebook a spiritual program that Venerable Bruno offered to a wife and mother of four children. He asked her to assist at Mass during the week when, without strain, this was possible; to spend fifteen minutes a day in some form of meditative prayer; to read one page each day from a spiritual book; and to make an examination of conscience when her hands were busy but her mind was free. The responses on Facebook were interesting. One comment may summarize many: "That's doable!" People understood the richness of this program and also that it was possible for them.

A Biblical Way of Praying the Mass

The same can be said of Venerable Bruno's way of praying the Mass. One need not read volumes to understand it. It adds no time to the day. It is easy to remember. It really is doable: you and I can pray the Mass this way.

And it makes all the difference when we are at Mass. It transforms our presence at Mass into a personally lived prayer. It opens the riches of every part of the Mass: the Introductory Rites, the Liturgy of the Word, the Liturgy of the Eucharist, and the Concluding Rites. It awakens that "Eucharistic amazement" of which Saint John Paul II spoke. It enkindles a growing love for the Eucharist until it truly becomes for us the "source and summit of the Christian life."

Do you desire to enter the Mass more deeply and to pray it from the heart? In the text we will explore, Venerable Bruno offers a sure path toward that deepening and that prayer.

This chapter recounts one person's story of the Mass. If you are reading this, it is because you, too, have your story of the Mass: the way in which God led you to it, the place it has held in your life, and the longing you feel to enter it more fully. Together we bless the Lord for the gift of the Mass through the years of our lives.

Wherever we find ourselves on the spiritual journey, Venerable Bruno's approach will help us pray the Mass with lively faith and with fruit. May his words bless us as they have so many before us.

2

Venerable Bruno and the Eucharist

*Preparing for Mass, I will think about God's
love for me. . . . In the thanksgiving after Mass,
I will think about our love for God.*

—Venerable Bruno Lanteri, age twenty-two

What place did the Eucharist have in Venerable Bruno's life? What was his story with the Mass? We will answer these questions through the witness of those who knew him and through his personal writings. The answers supply the context for his approach to the Mass and will help us understand it more deeply.

A first witness is Oblate Father Michele Valmino, a contemporary of Venerable Bruno. As a young man, Michele studied medicine. His studies were interrupted, however, when he joined Napoleon's armies and fought in Italy and Spain. Taken prisoner, he was sent to the Canary Islands. Through indiscriminate reading and his soldier's lifestyle, Michele lost all faith. After Napoleon's fall, he returned to his hometown of Carignano in Italy. When his parents died, he passed his days in hunting and caring for his garden.

A Biblical Way of Praying the Mass

Friends urged him to attend a parish mission given by the Oblates of the Virgin Mary. Reluctantly, and to please them, he went. A talk on the Passion of Christ touched his heart, and he returned to his faith. Ten years later, Michele joined the Oblates and was ordained a priest.

Michele's first three years with the Oblates coincided with Venerable Bruno's final three years of life. Perhaps because of his medical background, he was close to Venerable Bruno in those years of his physical struggles and final illness. Memories of those days remained with Michele throughout his life.

Years later, he recalled a time when he read from Saint Thomas Aquinas to Venerable Bruno: "He very much liked to hear others speak to him about the adorable Mystery of the Eucharist. In this regard, I remember that once I was in his room, and he was seated at a small table. He had me read aloud various passages from St. Thomas concerning this Mystery. After I had read for some time, I turned toward where he was seated to ask him something, and I saw the joy in his face, lit with a lively reddish color. It made a great impression on me because I had never seen him like this before."[7]

Largely confined because of illness, Venerable Bruno had a chapel made in the room next to his. Michele affirmed that "the Reverend Father Lanteri was deeply devoted to the Blessed Sacrament, and therefore desired that it be constantly reserved in the internal chapel of our house in Pinerolo. The chapel was adjacent to his room, and so that he might adore the Lord more frequently, especially in time of illness, he had a small window made in his room through which he could see the altar of this chapel. Through that window, he adored the Lord almost

---

[7] Timothy Gallagher, O.M.V., *Begin Again: The Life and Spiritual Legacy of Bruno Lanteri* (New York: Crossroad, 2013), 219.

continually in his last illness since the window was situated directly in front of his bed."[8]

In his final months, Bruno's desire to celebrate Mass conflicted with his physical weakness. Valmino remembered, "During his last illness, as long as he was able, he received the Eucharist daily, and with great consolation. As regards Holy Mass, he celebrated it daily with much devotion, and I do not recall that he ever failed to celebrate it unless he was gravely ill. Rather, one morning, some time before his last illness, though he was so ill that he could hardly stand, he desired nonetheless to celebrate Mass. But when he reached the first reading, he collapsed, and we had to divest him of the sacred vestments and take him back to his room."[9]

Another witness, twenty-one-year-old Brother Pietro Gardetti, who assisted Bruno in these months, later wrote, "Before going to bed I would pass by his room to ask him if he wanted anything. At times he would ask for some help, at times for nothing, telling me that he was greatly consoled because the Holy Father had granted him permission to have the Blessed Sacrament close to him."[10]

The same brother affirmed that "in his illness, he always wished to maintain his times of prayer, even when he was very weak. The two of us would say the prayers together, and the Rosary. When he drifted into sleep, I would not disturb him, and continued by myself. When he realized this, he would reprimand me for not waking him. When I read the *Visits to the Most Blessed Sacrament* of Blessed Liguori at 11:45 in the morning, he always tried, as best he could, to listen, telling me, 'This is worth more than all the rest.'"[11]

---

[8] Ibid.
[9] Ibid.
[10] Ibid., 219–220.
[11] Ibid., 236.

A Biblical Way of Praying the Mass

Like Father Valmino, Brother Pietro witnessed Bruno's struggle to celebrate Mass in those last months: "For some time, he had not been able to celebrate Holy Mass because he was so weak. One day he told me that he hoped to celebrate it on the day of St. Joseph. On the day of St. Joseph, he began the Mass and continued until he read the Gospel. After that, he rested for a short while seated on a chair. Then he continued to the end, and told me that St. Joseph had given him the grace he desired."[12]

Venerable Bruno's love for the Eucharist marked his whole life. Twenty years earlier, knowing that he risked death, Bruno defended Pope Pius VII, whom Napoleon had imprisoned. Bruno was arrested, interrogated, and by order of Napoleon, forcibly removed from priestly ministry and banished to an isolated country residence. During the three years of his exile, Bruno grew closer to the Eucharist.

Father Luigi Craveri, a disciple and frequent visitor, recalled that, "in the years he spent withdrawn there, I visited him more often than before and always returned from our conversations warmed by the encouragement he gave and with greater desire for the good. It was then that I came to admire more deeply, and with many confirmations, the great degree to which the theological and moral virtues were at work in that soul."[13]

With regard to the Eucharist, "he nourished his love for God in the time he spent before the Blessed Sacrament, and, during the years he spent in exile, meditated deeply on the things of God through the writings of St. Bonaventure with such savor and penetration that he said he had never known so much of God as after reading those sublime writings; consequently, I do not doubt that he reached the highest levels of contemplation, and I have

[12] Ibid., 229.
[13] Ibid., 95.

seen that he could discern the degrees and nature of such prayer with great ease."[14]

Throughout his life, Venerable Bruno urged others to draw close to the Eucharist. Two letters of spiritual direction, one to a laywoman and another to a layman, will suffice.

To Gabriella, a wife and mother, he writes:

> Your letter just arrived; I was glad to receive it, and it gave me real joy. I am happy to hear that your trip went well and that your whole family is in good health.... And it gives me greater happiness still to know that Father Ferrero is already there with you. It is important, then, to begin immediately to arrange with him for receiving Communion and to do so as often as you can.[15]

Venerable Bruno rejoices that Gabriella's family is well, but even more that the Eucharist is now available to her. In a time when Communion was often received only once a year, he encourages Gabriella to attend Mass and receive Communion as frequently as her responsibilities permit.

To Leopoldo, a husband and father, active in the Church but prone to lose heart, Bruno writes:

> In your letter I sense discouragement in the service of God. For God's sake, guard against this as there is no enemy more to be feared than this. A holy tenacity in the faithful practice of your ordinary exercises of the spiritual life, especially in

---

[14] Ibid., 95–96.

[15] Paolo Calliari, O.M.V., ed., *Carteggio del Venerabile Padre Pio Bruno Lanteri (1759–1830), fondatore della Congregazione degli Oblati di Maria Vergine* (Turin: Editrice Lanteri, 1976), 2, 208.

meditation and spiritual reading, will always be a source of great blessings for you. Add to this a weekly practice of the Sacrament of Penance and more than weekly Holy Communion, with a firm and invincible resolution always to begin again and to hope ever more firmly in God, and I guarantee you safety from major failings.[16]

Warmly, insistently, vigorously, and from deep personal experience and conviction, Venerable Bruno invites this man and woman — and us — to draw near the Eucharist.

How was this love for the Eucharist born in Bruno? Whence did it spring? Its remote origins lie in the Catholic upbringing his parents gave him, his mother in his first years and, above all, his father after his mother's early death. This love is apparent in Bruno's earliest writings and especially in a spiritual program he composed at age twenty-two. In these pages, the young Bruno's desire to live the Mass well is evident. "I will remember," he writes, "that the Sacrifice of the Mass is the same as that of Calvary in an unbloody manner."[17]

In these same pages, as ordination draws near, Bruno reflects that

the Mass is a prayer raised to the Holy Trinity by the whole human race, by the Church militant, suffering, and glorious, to present the most weighty and important matters of the world, and the priest is the mediator of this. The Mass represents the life and Last Supper of Jesus Christ; it is his same Sacrifice. When it is offered with due devotion, we are absolved from all our faults as if we had never committed

---

[16] *Carteggio*, 2, 161.

[17] Timothy Gallagher, O.M.V., ed., *Un'esperienza dello Spirito. Pio Bruno Lanteri: Il suo carisma nelle sue parole* (Cuneo: AGA, 1989), 78.

them. At Mass, we should imagine that we are in heaven and not on earth. Thousands of angels are present in adoration; they hold in esteem the hands of the priest."[18]

An awareness of the Mass as something great, profound, rich, fruitful, and infinitely desirable stirs in the young Bruno's heart.

Bruno then turns reflection into practice: "With regard to Communion, I plan to prepare the subject of my preparation and thanksgiving the evening before, to think of this immediately upon awaking, to do all of this with method and fidelity, and to return to these sentiments throughout the day and in my visit to the Blessed Sacrament."[19] When, years ago, I first read these lines, I found them a little intimidating! To choose on the preceding evening the thoughts and affections of the heart that will nourish the preparation for and thanksgiving after the next day's Communion: this was a level of preparation I had never considered. Clearly, Bruno's Communion will not just "happen" in the day. He knows, too, that such preparation will help his Communion bless the entire day.

How will he ready himself for Mass? "When I prepare, I will think about what will take place on the altar between me, the eternal Father, and his only-begotten Son. I will think about the four motives [adoration, contrition, thanksgiving, and supplication], and I will speak with each of the three Persons. I will ask for forgiveness of my sins, for the virtues I need, and I will ask Mary and Joseph to teach me how to conduct myself with Jesus. I will ask my Guardian Angel to assist me at the altar, and I will form the intention and the application of the Mass."[20]

---

[18] Gallagher, *Un'esperienza*, 80.
[19] Ibid., 63–64.
[20] Ibid., 74.

A Biblical Way of Praying the Mass

And after Mass? Bruno specifies this prayer in detail, "In my thanksgiving, I will adore him.... I will ask for an outpouring of graces, not only a few, but many and great, because God lavishes them upon us, especially the grace to be faithful to my vows and to practice virtue. Then I will pray for other general and special needs.... Finally, I will consecrate myself entirely, body and soul, to him. I will ask his blessing and strengthening before I go. I will especially commend sinners to him."[21]

Bruno plans to spend time daily before the Blessed Sacrament. "In my visit to the Blessed Sacrament," he writes, "I will make an act of faith, of adoration; I will ask for his help in the matters I face, or meditate on a phrase from the Our Father, or pray the Our Father with his aid, seeking the graces we ask for in it, or give thanks to him, or pray the 'We fly to thy patronage, O holy Mother of God.'"[22] This will be a prayer from the heart: "In the visit to the Blessed Sacrament ... pray, read, recite prayers, but stopping at times, with sighs, pauses, affections of the heart, and intervals for reflection."[23]

Daily Mass intentionally prepared and prolonged in prayer after and through the day, and daily time before the Blessed Sacrament with engagement of the heart: we touch here the center of Venerable Bruno's spiritual life. The Eucharist truly is for him "the source and summit of the Christian life."

Bruno outlines with care how he will prepare for Mass and how he will pray after it. But what about *during* the Mass? How will he pray in the Mass itself? What will fill his thoughts? What stirrings of heart will he seek?

Venerable Bruno, who plans his spiritual life so concretely, does not overlook this. In the same spiritual program, he crafts the

---

[21] Ibid., 74.
[22] Ibid., 78.
[23] Ibid., 72–73.

biblical approach to the Mass already mentioned.[24] For each part of the Mass, he chooses a biblical figure whose sentiments express those he desires in that part of the Mass. Our task in this book is to explore these figures, review how Venerable Bruno relates each to a specific moment in the Mass, and see how they can help us to pray that moment. Taken together, they offer a fruitful way to pray the Mass.

Venerable Bruno's manner of praying the Mass led him to a deep love for it. It can guide us to a similar love. Before turning to it, however, we must say a brief word about the *heart*, the primary focus of this approach.

[24] Ibid., 74. The original manuscript is found in the Archive of the Oblates of the Virgin Mary, series 2, document 6. It is also published in *Pio Bruno Lanteri: Scritti e Documenti d'Archivio* (Rome–Fossano: Edizioni Lanteri e Editrice Esperienze, 2002), 1, 568–569. With slight variations, Bruno wrote this text a second time for his Oblate priests: Gallagher, *Un'esperienza*, 124; *Pio Bruno Lanteri: Scritti e Documenti d'Archivio*, 3, 1854. For the manuscript of this second text, see Archive of the Oblates of the Virgin Mary, series 2, document 261.

3

A Heart-Centered Approach

Return to yourself! Return to your own heart! . . .
In the inner depths of your heart Christ lives.

—Saint Augustine

From the earliest times, God's people were taught to "love the Lord, your God, with your whole heart." They were to "take to heart these words" (Deut. 6:5–6). The psalmist prays, "With all my heart I seek you" (Ps. 119:10). On a mountaintop, Jesus would proclaim, "Blessed are the clean of heart, for they will see God" (Matt. 5:8). In that same discourse, he would add, "Where your treasure is, there also will your heart be" (Matt. 6:21).

Jesus, fulfilling the Old Testament, taught that "you shall love the Lord, your God, with all your heart, with all your soul, and with all your mind" (Matt. 22:37). To his anxious disciples, he said, "Do not let your hearts be troubled or afraid" (John 14:27). Paul urged the Philippians to bring their needs to God in prayer, adding, "Then the peace of God that surpasses all understanding will guard your hearts and minds in Christ Jesus" (4:7).

Over and over, in the Old Testament and in the New, Scripture speaks of the heart. What is the heart? Why is it so important? How does it relate to prayer?

A Biblical Way of Praying the Mass

When we pray in words or gestures, the *Catechism of the Catholic Church* affirms, it is the whole person who prays (CCC 2562). Yet, the *Catechism* continues, "in naming the source of prayer, Scripture sometimes speaks of the soul or the spirit, but most often of the heart (more than a thousand times). According to Scripture, it is the *heart* that prays" (2562). The emphasis is in the original.

A rich description of the heart follows:

- "The heart is the dwelling-place where I am and where I live."
- "According to the Semitic or Biblical expression, the heart is the place 'to which I withdraw.'"
- "The heart is our hidden center, beyond the grasp of our reason and of others."
- "Only the Spirit of God can fathom the human heart and know it fully."
- "The heart is the place of decision, deeper than our psychic drives."
- "It is the place of truth, where we choose life or death."
- "It is the place of encounter, because as image of God we live in relation."
- "It is the place of covenant." (CCC 2563)

How, then, can we pray the supreme prayer, the Mass, *from the heart*, from, with, and in this interior place to which we withdraw and in which we dwell, this hidden center of our being, this place of decision, of truth, of encounter, and of covenant?

Certainly, we can pray the Mass this way only if we understand it. We need a fundamental knowledge of the Mass, of its theological truth and of its structure. We need especially to understand its two key parts: the Liturgy of the Word, in which the Scriptures are proclaimed, and the Liturgy of the Eucharist, in which Jesus's sacrifice of himself is made present and we receive Communion.

This book will supply an essential presentation of these elements. We will never finish, however, learning about the Mass. I warmly invite you to pursue this learning further. Excellent resources exist. The twenty-two pages dedicated to the Holy Eucharist in *The Catechism of the Catholic Church* abundantly repay a thoughtful reading.[25] A brief web search for Catholic publications and digital materials on the Mass will provide many.[26]

But knowledge is not enough. "According to Scripture, it is the *heart* that prays," our "hidden center" where we encounter God. How can we pray the Mass with our *hearts*? How can our hearts engage ever more deeply in this prayer?

Since I learned of it forty-eight years ago, I have found no better way than that proposed by Venerable Bruno. Its entire focus is the heart. For each part of the Mass, Venerable Bruno urges us to seek "the sentiments and the heart" of some biblical figure.[27] In a later version of this text, he invites us to pray the Mass "with special attention to its principal parts so as to enkindle sentiments in keeping with each," again presenting these biblical figures.[28]

I have always appreciated the simplicity and practicality of this approach. For each key part of the Mass, the heart finds a concrete focus and a resting place. Venerable Bruno limits himself to the principal parts of the Mass. Because he does, his approach is well-suited to the heart. It can keep pace and transition gently from one part of the Mass to the next.

---

[25] Pages 334–356, nos. 1322-1419.

[26] For an ample selection of books on the Mass, visit Catholic Free Shipping, https://www.catholicfreeshipping.com/The-Catholic-Mass-Books-on-the-Catholic-Mass-s/266.htm. For an online resource, see the six-episode video series *Presence: The Mystery of the Eucharist* on FORMED from the Augustine Institute.

[27] Gallagher, *Un'esperienza*, 74.

[28] Ibid., 124.

A Biblical Way of Praying the Mass

What does this mean in practice? Do you wish to know how to enter the Mass with your heart? Seek the sentiments that filled Simeon's heart when he went to the Temple to meet Jesus. Do you desire to listen to the readings from your heart? Seek the sentiments in the hearts of those who listened to Jesus on the mountainside, by the lake, and in the Temple. Do you wish to pray the Consecration from your heart? Seek the sentiments of Jesus's own heart when he offered himself on the Cross. In each part of the Mass, our heart encounters a biblical heart upon which to focus and in which it finds an inexhaustible wellspring of love and appreciation. In a single glance, our heart penetrates the meaning of that moment of the Mass and lives it from its deepest center.

We turn now to the individual parts of the Mass as Venerable Bruno gives them and will explore how to live each from the heart.

4

Simeon Enters the Temple

Escape from your everyday business for a short while,
hide for a moment from your restless thoughts. . . .
Make a little time for God, and rest a while in him.

—Saint Anselm

Simeon rises and begins his day as usual. Outwardly, it is a day like many others. The sun shines, and it will be warm. He prays, eats his morning meal, and sets about his day. But his heart already knows that this day is different.

For so long, he has asked the Lord that, before he dies, he may see the Christ. Years have passed, and his desire has grown. But his prayer has not been answered.

Recently, however, he has sensed inner promptings, a consciousness that the day is approaching, and his longing has increased. To see the Christ! To see the anointed of the Lord with his own eyes! Everything in his long life of prayer, faithful service to God, and love of God and of his Law, has led to this point.

The hours pass, and suddenly Simeon knows that the time has come. Without delay, he prepares, leaves the house, and begins to walk. One street, then another—his slow, steady pace directs him unerringly to the Temple. The light of the Holy Spirit fills

A Biblical Way of Praying the Mass

his heart, leads him, guides him on his path, and Simeon follows unwaveringly. His heart thrills as each step hastens his encounter with the Christ of the Lord.

Now the Temple lies before him. Simeon approaches, enters … and he sees. He takes the child in his arms. The lifelong hunger of his heart is satisfied. Joy and gratitude fill his spirit. He blesses God and says, "Now, Master, you may let your servant go in peace … for my eyes have seen your salvation" (Luke 2:29–30).

You walk out the door of your home. You head to the car. You drive to church, park, and walk to the entrance of the church. Others, too, are approaching. You enter, walk down the aisle, find your place, genuflect, enter the pew, and kneel. The sacristan, priest, lector, and servers are preparing for Mass. In a few minutes, Mass will begin.

What stirs in your heart as you do this? What fills your thoughts? What desires do you feel? What sentiments awaken within?

Venerable Bruno writes, "When I enter the church, I will imagine that I see Simeon, who went in the Spirit to the Temple for the presentation and circumcision of Jesus, or I will imagine seeing some other fervent saint." Pause now for a moment and accompany Simeon on that day. Sit with him in the quiet of his home. Remember with him the many years of desire, the long-delayed fulfillment, the never-failing hope. Feel with him the thrill of awareness that today is the day. Open your heart, like his, to receive the Spirit's prompting. Walk with him through the streets. Draw near with him to the Temple. Enter the Temple with him. Feel with him the longing, the hope, the joy, and the love of the encounter that will now take place (see image 1).

In the communion of saints, speak with Simeon. Ask him to open his heart to you. Ask him to reveal to you what he felt that day. Then, ask him for a share in his sentiments as you prepare to meet Jesus in the Mass.

Could anything help more than this to enter Mass well?

As you walk, drive, or commute, and as you park, approach the church, enter, and settle in your pew, imagine that you see Simeon, "who went in the Spirit" to encounter the Lord. In the Mass about to begin, you will meet the same Lord.

Venerable Bruno then supplies a second help for entering Mass: "Or I will imagine seeing some other fervent saint." How did these holy men and women leave home and head to church for Mass? What filled their hearts and thoughts?

Saint Thérèse's parents, Saints Louis and Zélie Martin, began their day with Mass. Their daughter, Thérèse's sister Céline, writes, "Mother lived a life of deep piety. Every morning she assisted with my father at the 5:30 a.m. Mass; both of them went to Holy Communion as often as the custom permitted. In addition to that, on Sundays they assisted at the Solemn High Mass, and at Vespers."[29] Their biographer comments, "Whether they had been up late at night, or be Lent ever so hard—and the mother confessed that at times it cost her something—they rose at 5:00 a.m."[30]

Céline recounts of Louis, "Our father went daily to Mass, and also to Holy Communion as often as the custom of the time permitted. Accompanied by our mother, he left the house early, so much so that the neighbors used to say at the sound of the closing of the door: 'That is the holy Martin couple going to Mass, let us

---

[29] Céline Martin, *The Mother of the Little Flower: Zélie Martin 1831–1877* (Rockford, IL: TAN Books, 2005), 46.

[30] Stéphane-Joseph Piat, OFM, *The Story of a Family: The Home of St. Thérèse of Lisieux* (Rockford, IL: TAN Books, 1994), 151.

A Biblical Way of Praying the Mass

sleep some more!'"[31] When the family moved from Alençon to Lisieux, this practice continued: "At Lisieux it was most often at the Cathedral that my father assisted at Mass. The days on which he went to Holy Communion he generally remained silent on his return journey. 'I like to continue my conversation with Our Lord,' he used to say to us."[32]

Seven weeks before her painful death from cancer, Zélie wrote to her sister-in-law, "I had to start at 5 o'clock this morning in order to go to the first Mass. I was alone, as Louis was at Nocturnal Adoration. Finally, I called Marie to help me to dress. In church, I found it very hard to sit down, and to get on my knees. I could scarcely move without crying out; so I am not going back to High Mass again."[33]

Three weeks later, the eldest daughter, Marie, wrote to her aunt, Zélie's sister-in-law:

Since the beginning of the week, Mamma has been much worse. On Sunday, she still wanted to go to the first Mass; but she needed superhuman courage and had to make incredible efforts to get as far as the church. Every step she took seems to react on the pains in her neck. Sometimes she was obliged to stop in order to regain a little strength. When I saw that she was so exhausted, I begged her to return home, but she wanted to go on to the end, believing that the suffering was a passing attack. It was by no means that; on the contrary she had much trouble on the return journey, so she will not again be so imprudent.[34]

[31] Céline Martin, *The Father of the Little Flower: Louis Martin 1823–1894* (Rockford, IL: TAN Books, 2005), 4–5.
[32] Ibid., 5–6.
[33] Céline Martin, *The Mother of the Little Flower*, 98–99.
[34] Ibid., 101.

But it was not Zélie's last attempt. Twelve days later, three weeks before her death, Zélie sought once more to attend Mass. Marie writes, "Last Friday morning she went to the seven o'clock Mass, because it was the First Friday of the month. Papa helped her along, for without him she could not have gone at all. On arriving at the church, she admitted that if somebody were not with her, she would never have been able to push open the door of the church."[35]

Venerable Bruno invites us to "imagine seeing some fervent saint" as he or she looks forward to Mass, travels to church with this longing, enters the church, and prepares for Mass. What moved Saints Louis and Zélie to rise early and attend daily Mass? What drew them so strongly that nothing could hinder them from Mass?

What drew their daughter Saint Thérèse to Mass? What drew Saint Thomas More? Saint Elizabeth Seton? Saint John Paul II? Saint Gianna Beretta Molla? What filled their hearts as they left home and entered the church for Mass?

Venerable Bruno proposes an exercise of prayer. Could you pause for a moment to do this now as you read? Choose a saint whom you love and with whose life you are familiar. See this saint begin his or her day. Watch him or her arrange matters to make time for Mass. Leave home with this saint, accompany him or her to church, enter, and prepare for Mass with this saint. Ask him or her: What made you so desire Mass? What brought you to church? What did you seek? What did you find? Why did you go so often?

Ask for the same dispositions as you prepare for Mass.

> O God, you are my God—
> it is you I seek!

[35] Ibid., 105.

A Biblical Way of Praying the Mass

For you my body yearns;
   for you my soul thirsts,
In a land parched, lifeless,
   and without water.
I look to you in the sanctuary
   to see your power and glory. (Ps 63:1–2)

A Mass prepared with this desire will be prayed with faith, love, and spiritual fruit.

5

"O God, Be Merciful to Me"

How can I fear a God who is nothing but Mercy and Love?

—Saint Thérèse of Lisieux

Another man rises and begins his day. He is discouraged, and painful memories fill his heart. He cannot prevent them, and the day's activity grows harder. He sits at his tax collector's bench, and clients pass one after another. Gradually, the burden in his heart becomes unbearable. The morning passes, a brief meal, the afternoon begins … and he attempts to resume his work.

But the pain does not permit it. Finally, he stands motionless, unable to go on. Escapes of a certain kind are available, but he knows where they will lead. He has followed that path too often, and today's burden is in large part the result.

Another thought comes. God? Could he bring this pain to God? He? He who has harmed so many and so selfishly? Might God lift this burden? Could he ask this of God? A brief hesitation, and his decision is made.

He rises, leaves his work, and heads into the street. One street leads to another, and he nears his destination. He reaches it and enters the Temple. Others, too, come to pray, and they draw near the front. This man stays back, behind them all, at a distance (see image 2).

A Biblical Way of Praying the Mass

An awareness of his many sins floods his heart. He does not excuse them. He does not mitigate them. He accepts his responsibility. The man bows his head. His hand finds his breast, once and again. From his heart, with deep contrition, with utter sincerity, over and over he prays, "O God, be merciful to me a sinner" (Luke 18:13).

God loves that prayer. His mercy enfolds this man, and he is made clean. The man feels his burden lift, and joy fills his heart. He turns, leaves the Temple, and returns the way he came. This man, Jesus tells us, "went home justified" (Luke 18:14).

What stirs in our hearts when the priest says, "Brothers and sisters, let us acknowledge our sins, and so prepare ourselves to celebrate the sacred mysteries"? What fills our hearts when we say, "I confess to almighty God" and pray, "Lord, have mercy"?

Venerable Bruno writes, "In the Mass, at the Penitential Rite, I will seek the sentiments and the heart of the tax collector." He invites us to seek the sentiments of this tax collector as he prays in the Temple. Venerable Bruno urges us to desire a heart like his, aware of our need for forgiveness, willing to admit our responsibility, and above all, open to receive his infinite, warm, and loving mercy.

> Have mercy on me, God, in accord with your
> merciful love;
> in your abundant compassion blot out my
> transgressions.
> Thoroughly wash away my guilt;
> and from my sin cleanse me....
> Cleanse me with hyssop, that I may be pure;
> wash me, and I will be whiter than snow.
> (Ps. 51:3–4, 9)

Ask for a heart like this when you pray the Penitential Rite at Mass.

"O God, Be Merciful to Me"

Take a moment now to ponder the tax collector's prayer (Luke 18:9–14). Consider his heart: his sincerity, his openness, his contrition, his desire to change, and his trust in God's mercy. Pray for a heart like his. Then, with his same sentiments, slowly pray these words:

I confess to almighty God (the God whose infinite love and mercy we know)

and to you, my brothers and sisters (before whom also we accept our responsibility),

that I have greatly sinned (humble recognition, like the tax collector),

in my thoughts and in my words (how I have thought of others and how I have spoken),

in what I have done and in what I have failed to do (my actions and my omissions),

through my fault, through my fault (I accept my responsibility),

through my most grievous fault (and accept it again with a humble heart);

therefore I ask blessed Mary ever-Virgin (my heart lifts as I ponder her tender love),

all the Angels and Saints (my heart lifts further as I contemplate the multitude of angels and saints who love me),

and you, my brothers and sisters (I ask this, too, of those present here with me),

to pray for me to the Lord our God (with confidence, I ask for the prayers of all these).

A Biblical Way of Praying the Mass

∽

Now, with a heart like the tax collector's, pray the following words. Pause briefly at each invocation. The biblical verse cited may assist this meditation. As you pray, feel the healing grace of the God who is "nothing but mercy and love" (Saint Thérèse):

Lord, have mercy. ("Lord, you are good and forgiving, most loving to all who call on you" [Ps. 86:5].)

Lord, have mercy. ("With the Lord is mercy, with him is plenteous redemption" [Ps 130:7].)

Christ, have mercy. (A prayer to Jesus from the heart: "Lord, if you wish, you can make me clean" [Matt. 8:2].)

Christ, have mercy. (Again, from the heart: "Jesus, Son of David, have pity on me" [Mark 10:47].)

Lord, have mercy. ("God, who is rich in mercy ... brought us to life with Christ" [Eph. 2:4–5]. Our God is *rich in mercy*.)

Lord, have mercy. ("Let us confidently approach the throne of grace to receive mercy" [Heb. 4:16].)

Pray these invocations in this way, with these sentiments, when you are at Mass.

Sometimes, when I celebrate Mass and pray these invocations, they seem to me the heart of all prayer: "Lord, have mercy.... Christ, have mercy.... Lord, have mercy." In our helplessness, we turn again and again to God, asking for healing, love, blessing, and new hope. And God hears that prayer.

6

A Heart Filled with Praise

*Oh, what a great thing it is, and how consoling,
to serve as an instrument for God's glory!*

—Venerable Bruno Lanteri

I used to wonder why God wanted our praise. The joyful communion of love in the Trinity is complete: What could add to it?
What could our praise contribute? Why did it matter to praise God?

One Sunday, I received my answer. I had just celebrated the
11:00 a.m. Mass, and it was time for the announcements. As usual
with this Mass, the church was full. Beside me stood Deacon Tom,
much loved in the parish.

Deacon Tom was the "glue" that held things together on weekend Masses. He was present for all of them. He ensured that we
had servers, Eucharistic ministers, and lectors and that they knew
their roles. He prepared the chalice, the hosts, and the cruets and
set them on the table for the procession with the gifts. I had never
seen anyone work so diligently on his homilies, devoting hours and
hours to the task during the week. The people loved his preaching.

At this point, due to age and health, Deacon Tom had to re-
tire, and we shared this news at the Masses that weekend. Now,
as the 11:00 a.m. Mass ended, I read the scripted announcement

and then spoke my own words of appreciation. When I finished, the people stood and applauded, the kind of applause that goes on and on, when people want to show the sincerity and depth of their gratitude. Deacon Tom faced them, both embarrassed and moved.

The Mass ended, the final hymn was sung, and we processed out of the church. I stood there, greeting people as they exited. Every face was smiling, and many made comments such as "Nice Mass," "Wonderful Mass," and "Thank you for a lovely Mass."

When all had left, I walked back to the rectory thinking about what had just happened. Something dawned on me. The uplifted hearts and the smiles were linked to what took place just minutes before: we had expressed, from our hearts, gratitude to another and, in so doing, had become happy ourselves.

That, I understood, was why God wanted our praise: because when we praise God something joyful enters our hearts and our lives. In the Mass we pray, "You have no need of our praise, yet our desire to thank you is itself your gift" (Weekday Preface IV). Yes, God does not need our praise for his sake but desires it for ours, because when we praise God, our hearts receive love, grace, and joy.

Venerable Bruno writes, "At the Gloria, I will seek the sentiments and the heart of the Angels." When we pray the words, "Glory to God in the highest, and on earth peace to people of good will. We praise you, we bless you, we adore you, we glorify you," and the whole of this prayer of praise, Venerable Bruno invites us to do so with the sentiments and heart of the angels on the night when Christ was born in Bethlehem (Luke 2:13–14).

God has taken flesh and lies in a manger. The angel proclaims "good news of great joy that will be for all the people. For today in the city of David a savior has been born for you who is Messiah and Lord" (Luke 2:10–11). As the shepherds gaze in wonder, a multitude of angels fills the heavens and sings God's praise (see image 3). Our Gloria in the Mass praises God with their same words.

With what appreciation of God's work did the angels sing these words that night? With what understanding of the magnitude of the gift? With what joy? With what delight? With what desire to praise God for the immensity of his love? When you pray the Gloria at Mass, Venerable Bruno tells us, ask for their same sentiments. Ask for a heart like theirs, eager to proclaim God's praises.

Take a moment now to contemplate the angels' prayer. If you find it helpful, open the Bible and read Luke 2:8–14. Then visualize the scene: the dark of night, the flocks of sheep, the shepherds, the glory of God filling the heavens, the joyful proclamation of the angel, the song of the angelic choir. Feel the delight that inspires these words. Ask for a share in that joy. Then, with the "sentiments and heart" of these angels, slowly pray the Gloria:

Glory to God in the highest (raise your heart on high; let it express joyful praise of God),

and on earth peace to people of good will (ask for God's peace on this troubled earth).

We praise you (pause simply to recognize God's love and goodness),

we bless you (pronounce his name with love and reverence; bless him for his works of love),

we adore you (lift your heart in reverent and joyful adoration of his love, his goodness),

we glorify you (express your love for God, glorify him with your heart, your words, your life),

we give you thanks for your great glory (thank him for his saving work in the world and in your life),

Lord God, heavenly King (welcome him with love as Lord, as King in your life),

O God, almighty Father (open your heart to the love and power of our heavenly Father),

Lord Jesus Christ, Only Begotten Son (turn now to Jesus, our Lord, the beloved Son in whom the Father takes delight),

Lord God, Lamb of God, Son of the Father ("Behold, the Lamb of God" [John 1:36]: see the divine Lamb; behold him; draw near to him with confidence),

you take away the sins of the world, have mercy on us (ask with confidence for the mercy that *takes away* sin);

you take away the sins of the world, receive our prayer ("Everyone who asks, receives" [Matt. 7:8]; present your prayer with trust in his promise);

you are seated at the right hand of the Father, have mercy on us ("Therefore he is always able to save those who approach God through him, since he lives forever to make intercession for them" [Heb. 7:25]; ponder these words).

For you alone are the Holy one (acknowledge the unique holiness, goodness, and love of Jesus),

you alone are the Lord ("At the name of Jesus every knee should bend ... and every tongue confess that Jesus Christ is Lord" [Phil. 2:10–11]: profess him as the Lord of your life.),

you alone are the Most High ("you alone": give him this special, unequalled place in your life, in your heart.),

Jesus Christ (the Son, our Savior),

with the Holy Spirit (the Paraclete, the Advocate, the Consoler),

in the glory of God the Father (our loving Father in heaven).

Amen.

Venerable Bruno invites us to pray the Gloria in this way, from the heart, with these sentiments, when we are at Mass.

7

Hearts Raised in Supplication

Prayer stands before God as an honored ambassador.

—Saint John Chrysostom

Venerable Bruno's text then reads, "At the Prayers, I will seek the sentiments and the heart of an ambassador sent by the Church." By "Prayers" he intends the "Orations," the prayers that the priest pronounces in the name of the assembly: the Collect, the Prayer over the Gifts, and the Prayer after Communion.

When the priest prays these Orations, he is to seek the "sentiments and the heart of an ambassador sent by the Church," or as Bruno writes in a variant, those of a "legate." The priest gathers (thus, "Collect") the prayers of all and presents them to God. He serves as our "ambassador" or "legate" before God, bearing to God the desires, needs, hopes, sorrows, and joys of all present. We join with the priest as he lifts our prayers to God.

A tension arises between two nations. War threatens. Both nations know that armed conflict will bring disaster and untold suffering upon their people. Efforts are made to resolve the tension, but they are unavailing. Both nations arm and deploy their troops. War is imminent.

The government of one nation convenes in urgent session. Its members draft an equitable proposal for peace. An ambassador is named. His mission is announced to the other nation, which agrees to meet with him and consider the proposal. The ambassador boards a plane and travels to the other nation. Minute by minute, the media cover his travel, his arrival, and his meetings with the officials of the other nation. All other activity ceases. The people of both nations follow the unfolding reports, hanging on every word.

The ambassador speaks with the officials. His heart is charged with the importance of what he does. He knows that he carries the hopes and fears of so many. He knows that he is their spokesman. He knows the importance of the message he carries. He puts all of himself into this mission.

When the priest prays the Orations, Venerable Bruno says, *let him* pray them in this way, conscious that he is our ambassador, aware of the importance of what he does, knowing that he bears to God the hopes and fears of the people. And when the priest prays these Orations, *let us* hear them knowing the importance of what takes place, aware that the priest lifts our prayers, our needs, to God.

One afternoon, when I was stationed in Boston, I stopped at St. Anthony's Shrine to pray. In this downtown church, the Franciscans offer Masses, confessions, and Eucharistic Adoration for the many who work there. Eucharistic Adoration was in progress, and people were scattered throughout the church in silent prayer. A priest was hearing confessions, and people waited their turn, entering the confessional one by one.

Suddenly, a disturbance arose in the rear of the church. In-stinctively, all turned to see what was happening. On the right was a statue of the Infant Jesus. Rows of candles stood before it. A young man in his late teens, powerful in physique, was kneeling in the aisle before the statue. He was praying out loud in his own language, swaying a little with the intensity of his prayer, clearly pouring out a prayer of anguish, moved by some great need.

A security guard approached and gently suggested that the young man move out of the aisle and pray less loudly. The young man never even saw him, never even heard him. He had no attention for anything but this prayer from his heart.

Wisely, the guard moved away. All in the church returned to their prayer.

I have often thought of that young man's prayer and wished to pray like that, from the heart.

After the Gloria, the priest says, "Let us pray." A brief time of silence follows. In this time, we present to God the needs of our hearts, the many prayers we desire to express. Then the priest, as our ambassador, gathers our prayers and lifts them to God through the Collect of the Mass. Venerable Bruno invites us to join our hearts to this prayer, knowing that, through it, our prayers rise to God.

Pray this Collect now, slowly and from the heart:

Almighty and merciful God (we lift our heart to you, loving Father, who are infinitely powerful and whose mercy knows no limits),

graciously keep from us all adversity (we pray for free-dom from physical, moral, and spiritual harm),

so that, unhindered in mind and body alike (not weighed down by burdens of mind and body),

we may pursue in freedom of heart (our hearts may be truly free to pursue what is most important: a great grace!)

the things that are yours (love of God, love of neighbor, doing God's will, living our vocations, eternal life; we ask for freedom to live in the way God desires, in the light of his Word),

Through our Lord Jesus Christ, your Son,
who lives and reigns with you in the unity of the Holy Spirit,

one God, for ever and ever.
R. Amen.[36]

These Orations are rich and repay attention. They supply words to express what we might otherwise struggle to say to God. They remind us of truths and express desires fundamental to our faith and our spiritual lives. Venerable Bruno invites us to pray these Orations — the Collect, the Prayer over the Gifts, and the Prayer after Communion — with the priest and in this way: from our hearts.

---

[36] Collect for the Thirty-Second Sunday of Ordinary Time.

8

A Disciple's Heart

Let God's Word enter your very being.
Let it take possession of your desires and
your whole way of life. Feed on goodness,
and your soul will delight in its richness.

—Saint Bernard of Clairvaux

He saw the crowds that pressed about him. He climbed the mountain, found an open space, and sat. His disciples followed and gathered around him. "When he sat down, his disciples came to him. And he opened his mouth and taught them" (Matt. 5:1–2, RSVCE). He spoke at length, and they listened, eager to hear his words, warmed by his wisdom, moved by his encouragement. Hours passed, and none left. He finished, and they departed, renewed and filled with hope.

Again the crowds gathered. This time, too, "the people pressed upon him to hear the word of God" (Luke 5:1, RSVCE). Hemmed in by their numbers, he stepped into a boat and continued to teach. The people were silent, intent upon his words. They felt the power of his message. They loved its freshness, the new horizons it opened.

A Biblical Way of Praying the Mass

The morning advanced, and no one moved. All listened until he ceased to speak.

The crowds searched for him and found him in Capernaum. He spoke of a bread of life that he would give, and he said that whoever would eat his flesh and drink his blood would have eternal life. Some found this hard to accept and withdrew. He turned to the Twelve and asked, "Do you also want to leave?" "Simon Peter answered him, 'Master, to whom shall we go? You have the words of eternal life'" (John 6:67–68). You have the *words of eternal life*, words that are spirit and life (John 6:63), words of power, truth, light, and love. To whom else shall we go? To whom else shall we listen?

Jerusalem was filled with pilgrims for the feast of Tabernacles. He entered the Temple and taught openly. Great numbers listened, among them the guards sent to arrest him. These returned to the chief priests and Pharisees empty-handed. Asked why they had not brought him, the guards replied, "No man ever spoke like this man!" (John 7:46, RSVCE). No, no man ever spoke, has ever spoken like this man! The guards felt the power of his words, words like none they had ever heard. Together with the crowd, they listened, fascinated, moved, captivated by the richness of his teaching.

Day after day, he entered the Temple and sat. The people assembled around him, and he taught them. Each day, the scene of deeply attentive people repeated: "All the people hung upon his words" (Luke 19:48, RSVCE). *They hung upon his words*, forgetful of all else, desiring only to absorb what he said. Their hearts were stirred. They departed thoughtful, their faith enlivened and their hearts kindled with new desire for God.

Venerable Bruno writes, "At the Readings and Gospel, I will seek the sentiments and the heart of a disciple." When the First Reading, the Second, and the Gospel are proclaimed, ask for a heart like those of the disciples who heard Jesus on the mountain, by the lakeshore, and in the Temple. Listen as they did, with the same deep attention, undivided heart, and receptivity: when his Word is read at Mass, Jesus speaks to you just as he did to them.

"In the sacred books the Father who is in heaven meets His children with great love and speaks with them."[37] And again, "When the Sacred Scriptures are read in the Church, God himself speaks to his people, and Christ, present in his word, proclaims the Gospel."[38] As he spoke to the crowds then, Jesus now speaks to us in the Mass. And so, Venerable Bruno urges, ask for a listening heart like those of the disciples in the Gospels.

As mentioned earlier, when I was an assistant to our novice master, he asked me to speak to the novices on Sacred Scripture in the spiritual life. It was my first assignment after ordination, and as you can imagine, I put my heart into it. I have always considered the preparation of those talks one of the great graces of my priesthood. I spent hours in the library exploring Church texts about Scripture. I read the writings of the Fathers and those of various saints on the

---

[37] Second Vatican Council, Dogmatic Constitution on Divine Revelation *Dei Verbum* (November 18, 1965), no. 21.
[38] *General Instruction of the Roman Missal*, 29.

same theme. I came to love and revere Scripture in a new way as I saw it through the eyes of the Church and these figures of holiness.

I grasped more deeply the truth just described: that the scenes on the mountainside, on the lakeshore, and in the Temple are renewed in the Mass. Jesus is again among us, speaking his word to us. I understood anew Venerable Bruno's invitation to hear the scriptural readings at Mass with a disciple's heart.

In August 1989, I watched the television coverage of the first World Youth Day outside of Rome. A crowd of six hundred thousand young people gathered for the final Mass, held on open ground outside Santiago de Compostela in Spain. They sat in a semicircle, forming an enormous human amphitheater on the hillside above the platform with the altar.

The theme chosen for the event was "I am the way, the truth, and the life," from the Gospel of John (14:6). The Mass began. After the Readings and the Gospel were proclaimed, John Paul II began his homily. At one point, he cited John 14:6. I will never forget how he said these words and their impact on the thousands of young people before him.

With great feeling and with his deep, resonant voice, he pronounced Jesus's words: "I am the way!" A sustained applause arose from the assembly. Then, "And the truth!" Once more, applause. Finally, "And the life!" Again, lengthy applause. Like them, I was moved as I watched and listened. I had heard these words many times, but said by this man, in this way, with this conviction, and from his heart, Jesus's words were powerful. I felt that I had glimpsed what those who heard Jesus speak must have experienced.

"At the Readings and Gospel, I will seek the sentiments and the heart of a disciple." Love, author Simone Weil writes, consists of knowing how to look at another "in a certain way." She explains, "This way of looking is first of all attentive. The soul empties itself of all its own contents in order to receive into itself the being it is looking at, just as he is, in all his truth."[39] A heart attentive in this way, completely available, wholly centered on Jesus's Word as it is proclaimed—such is the heart that Venerable Bruno enjoins us to seek when the Scriptures are read at Mass.

I invite you now, for a moment, to listen to the Gospel in this way. If you do so outside of Mass, you will more likely do it during Mass. For this listening, I propose the Gospel passage with which we opened this chapter: Matthew 5:1–10, the beginning of the Sermon on the Mount.

Be there on the mountainside (see image 4). Take your place close to Jesus. See the great crowd around you, eager to listen. Slowly read the words, and hear Jesus say them personally *to you*. Pause after each beatitude to consider it briefly: What does it mean? What is Jesus saying to you?

When he saw the crowds, he went up the mountain, and after he had sat down, his disciples came to him (you are seated there among them).

He began to teach them, saying:

Blessed are the poor in spirit (poor in spirit: humble, knowing our need for God, trusting in him),

for theirs is the kingdom of heaven.

Blessed are they who mourn (mourn over sin and evil),

for they will be comforted.

---

[39] Simone Weil, *Waiting for God* (San Francisco: Harper & Row, 1992), 114.

A Biblical Way of Praying the Mass

Blessed are the meek (meek: gentle, not quick to take offense, patient),

for they will inherit the land.

Blessed are they who hunger and thirst for righteousness (hunger and thirst for holiness, for new closeness to God),

for they will be satisfied.

Blessed are the merciful (the practice of the corporal and spiritual works of mercy),

for they will be shown mercy.

Blessed are the clean of heart (interiorly clean, pure, without duplicity),

for they will see God.

Blessed are the peacemakers (those who reconcile people with each other and with God),

for they will be called children of God.

Blessed are they who are persecuted for the sake of righteousness (those who suffer for their fidelity to Christ),

for theirs is the kingdom of heaven.

If you listen to the readings at Mass in this way, with a disciple's heart, then Jesus's Word will become for you, as the Second Vatican Council affirms, a "strength of faith," a "food of the soul," and a "pure and everlasting source of spiritual life."[40]

---

[40] *Dei Verbum*, no. 21.

9

The Courage of the Martyrs

When it is necessary to think, speak, and labor
for God, to give my very life, let all be lost, let
whatever will happen, happen; this I must do.

—Venerable Bruno Lanteri

Justin and his companions stood before the Roman prefect Rusticus. It was the year 165, and Marcus Aurelius was emperor of Rome.

Rusticus said to Justin, "Above all, have faith in the gods and obey the emperors."[41]

Justin replied, "We cannot be accused or condemned for obeying the commands of our Savior, Jesus Christ."

Rusticus said, "What system of teaching do you profess?"

Justin answered, "I have tried to learn about every system, but I have accepted the true doctrines of the Christians, though these are not approved by those who are held fast by error."

Rusticus then said, "Are those doctrines approved by you, wretch that you are?"

---

[41] This and the subsequent quotations are from the *Acts of the Martyrdom of Saint Justin and His Companion Saints*, as found in *The Liturgy of the Hours* (New York: Catholic Book Publishing, 1975), 3:1854–1856.

A Biblical Way of Praying the Mass

Justin said, "Yes, for I follow them with their correct teaching."

Rusticus asked, "What sort of teaching is that?"

Justin, in his name and that of his companions, professed his faith, "Worship the God of the Christians. We hold him to be from the beginning the one Creator and Maker of the whole creation, of things seen and unseen. We worship also the Lord Jesus Christ, the Son of God. He was foretold by the prophets as the future herald of salvation for the human race and the teacher of distinguished disciples. For myself, since I am a human being, I consider that what I say is insignificant in comparison with this infinite godhead. I acknowledge the existence of a prophetic power, for the one I have just spoken of as the Son of God was the subject of prophecy. I know that the prophets were inspired from above when they spoke of his coming among men."

Rusticus said, "You are a Christian, then?"

Justin answered, "Yes, I am a Christian."

Rusticus replied, "You are called a learned man and think you know what is true teaching. Listen: if you were scourged and beheaded, are you convinced that you would go up to heaven?"

Justin said, "I hope that I shall enter God's house if I suffer in that way. For I know that God's favor is stored up until the end of the whole world for all who have lived good lives."

Rusticus answered, "Do you have an idea that you will go up to heaven to receive some suitable reward?"

Justin replied, "It is not an idea that I have; it is something I know well and hold to be most certain."

Rusticus then lost patience. He said, "Now let us come to the point at issue, which is necessary and urgent. Gather around then and with one accord offer sacrifice to the gods."

Justin answered, "No one who is right-thinking stoops from true worship to false worship."

Rusticus said, "If you do not do as you are commanded you will be tortured without mercy."

Justin replied, "We hope to suffer torment for the sake of our Lord Jesus Christ, and so be saved. For this will bring us salvation and confidence as we stand before the more terrible and universal judgment-seat of our Lord and Savior."

Justin's companions also spoke, "Do what you will. We are Christians; we do not offer sacrifice to idols."

Rusticus then passed sentence, and their martyrdom followed. The account concludes, "They were beheaded, and so fulfilled their witness of martyrdom in confessing their faith in the Savior." We know them today as Saint Justin Martyr and companions.

Venerable Bruno writes, "At the Profession of Faith, I will seek the sentiments and the heart of the martyrs." At Mass, when you say "I believe in one God. . . . I believe in one Lord Jesus Christ. . . . I believe in one, holy, catholic, and apostolic Church. . . . I look forward to the resurrection of the dead and the life of the world to come," profess this, proclaim this, affirm this, Venerable Bruno urges, with the sentiments and heart of a martyr. Say it as a martyr would, from your heart, with all your being, ready to lay your life on the line for the faith you express (see image 5).

I find that Venerable Bruno's counsel transforms how I pray the Profession of Faith. This Profession comes alive. It acquires new meaning. I grasp its importance and its solemnity. The memory of martyrs such as Justin awakens a desire to pray it in this way.

Read once again the account of Saint Justin Martyr. Hear and ponder his courageous profession of faith, his steadfastness, and his readiness to witness to Jesus.

Ask the Lord for a heart like Saint Justin's and that of other martyrs, past and present, who professed their faith with similar

A Biblical Way of Praying the Mass

courage. Then, slowly pray the Niceno-Constantinopolitan Creed that we say at Mass. As you pray, pause briefly at each truth you express. Let its meaning fill your heart. Renew your faith in it.

I believe in one God,

the Father almighty (I believe in you, God the Father, God my father),

maker of heaven and earth (I believe in you as Creator),

of all things visible and invisible.

I believe in one Lord Jesus Christ (I believe in you, Jesus, the Christ, and my Lord),

the Only Begotten Son of God,

born of the Father before all ages.

God from God, Light from Light,

true God from true God (I believe that you, Jesus, are true God),

begotten, not made, consubstantial with the Father;

through him all things were made.

For us men and for our salvation (I believe that you are my Savior)

he came down from heaven,

and by the Holy Spirit was incarnate (I believe in your Incarnation)

of the Virgin Mary (I believe that you took flesh through Mary),

and became man.

For our sake he was crucified under Pontius Pilate,

he suffered death and was buried (I believe that you died for our salvation),

and rose again on the third day (I believe in your Resurrection from the dead in power and glory)

in accordance with the Scriptures.

He ascended into heaven

and is seated at the right hand of the Father (I believe in your Ascension, that you were taken up to heaven).

He will come again in glory

to judge the living and the dead (I believe in your Second Coming at the end of time)

and his kingdom will have no end.

I believe in the Holy Spirit, the Lord, the giver of life (I believe in you, God the Holy Spirit, "Paraclete, Gift of God, living Fountain, Fire, Love, spiritual Anointing" [*Veni Creator Spiritus*]),

who proceeds from the Father and the Son,

who with the Father and the Son is adored and glorified,

who has spoken through the prophets.

I believe in one, holy, catholic and apostolic Church (I believe that you founded the Catholic Church, the Spouse of the Lamb, our Mother).

I confess one Baptism for the forgiveness of sins (I believe in the grace and power of Baptism, of my Baptism)

and I look forward to the resurrection of the dead

and the life of the world to come. Amen. (I believe in eternal life).

Pray the Profession of Faith like this at Mass.

10

Bread, Wine, and the Gift of Self

*I felt myself renewed to my very depths by Him, ready for a
new life, for duty, for the work intended by His Providence.
I gave myself without reserve, and I gave him the future.*

—Servant of God Elisabeth Leseur

Abram has just returned victorious from battle, and a mysterious
figure comes to meet him (see image 6). This man, Melchizedek,
is a king and a priest. He brings bread and wine. His ancestry is
not given; he simply appears on the biblical scene. When he meets
Abram, Melchizedek says, "Blessed be Abram by God Most High,
the creator of heaven and earth; and blessed be God Most High,
who delivered your foes into your hand" (Gen. 14:19–20). Abram
gives him a tithe of all he possesses.

As salvation history and the writing of the Bible continue,
Melchizedek is not forgotten. He is evoked in the Psalms, when
the king is told that, "The LORD has sworn and will not waver:
'Like Melchizedek, you are a priest forever'" (110:4).

Melchizedek reappears in the New Testament where he is seen
as a foreshadowing of Christ, our king and priest. In the Letter to
the Hebrews, we read, "This 'Melchizedek, king of Salem and priest
of God Most High,' 'met Abraham as he returned from his defeat of

the kings' and 'blessed him.' And Abraham apportioned to him 'a tenth of everything.' His name first means righteous king, and he was also 'king of Salem,' that is, king of peace. Without father, mother, or ancestry, without beginning of days or end of life, thus made to resemble the Son of God, he remains a priest forever" (7:1–3).

Nothing is said of Melchizedek's human origins, nothing of his death, nothing of the passing of his priesthood. He is a king, and he is a priest; he arises outside the Levitical priesthood. Scripture understands Melchizedek, therefore, as a prefiguration of the fullness of priesthood in Jesus: "Son though he was, he learned obedience from what he suffered; and when he was made perfect, he became the source of eternal salvation for all who obey him, declared by God high priest according to the order of Melchizedek" (Heb. 5:8–10).

Venerable Bruno writes, "At the Preparation of the Gifts, I will seek the sentiments and the heart of Melchizedek." In a variant of this text, he speaks of "the sentiments of the priest Melchizedek," emphasizing the priestly character of this man and even more of Christ, the High Priest who fulfills what Melchizedek prefigures.[42] At this point in the Mass, the Preparation of the Gifts, when the sacrificial offerings are prepared, Venerable Bruno invites us to seek *the heart of a priest.*

Vatican II teaches that *we are all priests* according to the common priesthood of the faithful.[43] You are a priest. The sacrament of Baptism consecrates the recipient to the common priesthood of the faithful; building on this, the sacrament of Holy Orders consecrates the recipient to the ministerial priesthood. These two forms of priesthood — the priesthood of the faithful and the ministerial

---

[42] Gallagher, *Un'esperienza,* 124.
[43] *Lumen Gentium,* no. 10.

priesthood—differ, the council explains, in essence, but each is a real priesthood, a sharing in the one priesthood of Christ.[44]

I invite you to read these next words slowly and thoughtfully. They are too rich in content for a quick glance. If we assimilate what the council says here, it will change forever the way we participate at Mass:

The baptized, by regeneration and the anointing of the Holy Spirit (it is through our Baptism that we share in the priesthood of Christ),

are consecrated as a spiritual house and a holy priesthood (as the baptized, we are consecrated as priests, called to be holy as we live the priesthood of the faithful)

in order that through all those works which are those of the Christian (through living in the world: in our family, in our work, in our engagement with the world)

they may offer spiritual sacrifices (as priests, through our lives as Christians in the world, we offer spiritual sacrifices to God)

and proclaim the power of him who has called them out of darkness into his marvelous light (our lives are to proclaim Christ to others: our priesthood of the faithful is directed also to this proclamation to the world).

Therefore all the disciples of Christ, persevering in prayer and praising God (*all* the disciples of Christ: this is your call, to persevere in prayer and, by the way you live, to praise God),

should present themselves as a living sacrifice (this is the sacrifice you offer through your priesthood of the faithful: *yourself, your own life*, offered to God),

holy and pleasing to God" (this sacrifice of your life is to be holy, pleasing in God's sight).[45]

---

[44] Ibid.
[45] Ibid.

A Biblical Way of Praying the Mass

Abstract theology? Remote speculative considerations? No. Your priesthood lies at the heart of your life and reveals the deepest meaning of your participation in the Mass. Two hundred fifty years ago, Venerable Bruno urged us to understand and, above all, to live this priesthood at Mass: "At the Preparation of the Gifts, I will seek the sentiments and the heart of the priest Melchizedek."[46]

We seek the sentiments and the heart of Melchizedek, the priest, who foreshadows the Eternal Priest, Jesus, who has called us to share in his priesthood. Because we are priests, we are called *to offer sacrifice to God*, the sacrifice of our lives, of all that we are and do: "Therefore all the disciples of Christ, persevering in prayer and praising God, should present themselves as a living sacrifice, holy and pleasing to God."

What, then, does it mean to live the Preparation of the Gifts with the heart of the priest Melchizedek? When you are at Mass, many things stir in your heart: family issues, financial matters, spiritual concerns, gratitude for blessings received, troubling responsibilities, physical burdens, uncertainties about the future, prayers for those you love, for the Church, and for the world. Present yourself, present all this to God as "a living sacrifice, holy and pleasing" to him. Unite the sacrifice of your life with the sacrifice of Christ that will soon be present on the altar. Joined to his sacrifice, the sacrifice of your life gains immense value and richness before God.

At the Preparation of the Gifts, remember Melchizedek. Above all, remember Jesus, the high priest according to the order of Melchizedek. Remember his priestly heart. Remember his sacrifice of himself. Ask for a heart like his. Exercise your priesthood. Offer

---

[46] I am presenting his words in the light of Vatican II and as applied to the laity. The ordained priest will receive these words in the light of his ministerial priesthood.

the living sacrifice of your life, with all its joys and trials. This offering will bring you into the heart of the Mass.

∞

Take a moment and pray:

> God, my loving Father, when the priest and servers prepare the altar and place the sacred vessels upon it, grant me the Heart of Jesus, our High Priest according to the order of Melchizedek. Help me prepare to offer my life with all its joys and struggles to you as "a living sacrifice, holy and pleasing" in your sight.
>
> Father, when the gifts are brought in procession, help me to present, with them, my life, my desire to grow closer to you, my family, my hopes, my fears, my concerns of health, the financial issues I face, and help me to offer all of this with Jesus in this Mass.
>
> Father, when the priest says over the bread and wine, "Blessed are you, Lord God of all creation, for through your goodness we have received the bread we offer you … the wine we offer you …," grant me a heart like that of Jesus, who offers himself in the form of bread and wine. I join the offering of my life with that of Jesus on the altar, and by your grace, I make this offering from my heart.
>
> Father, when the priest washes his hands, I ask that you wash and cleanse me too. I ask for a heart made pure, a heart prepared to pray the Eucharistic Prayer, to live the Consecration, and to receive the Communion that will follow.
>
> Father, when the priest says, "Pray, brothers and sisters, that my sacrifice and yours may be acceptable to God, the almighty Father," help me to respond from my heart, "May the Lord accept the sacrifice at your hands for the praise

and glory of his name, for our good, and the good of all his holy Church." Make my sacrifice, too, the offering of my life, acceptable to you.

At the Preparation of the Gifts, seek the priestly sentiments and heart of Jesus, our High Priest according to the order of Melchizedek.

1. Simeon in the Temple

2. The Tax Collector and the Pharisee

3. The Angels on Christmas Night

4. Jesus Teaches the People

5. The Faith of the Martyrs

6. The Meeting of Abram and Melchizedek

7. The Heavenly Court

8. Jesus Gives His Life for Us

9. The Lamb of God

10. Jesus Sends the Apostles

11

Before the Throne of God

*It was revealed to Abba Anthony in his desert that there
was one who was his equal in the city. He was a doctor by
profession, and whatever he had beyond his needs he gave to
the poor, and every day he sang the Sanctus with the angels.*

— *The Sayings of the Desert Fathers*

In my family, we all knew that my mother liked Antonio Vivaldi's
Gloria. Her regard for it awakened a similar appreciation in us,
and we listened to it many times. She once said that when she
thought of the singing in heaven — see, for example, Revelation
14:2–3 — she thought that it would be like this *Gloria*.

I remember her words whenever I listen to Vivaldi's *Gloria*. I
believe she is right: its music offers a glimpse of what it will mean
to praise God in eternal life. The beauty of this Gloria, the joy, the
exuberance, the delight it expresses, and its soul-stirring richness
speak of the gratitude with which angels and saints praise God in
heaven.

I invite you now to pause in your reading, go on YouTube, and
listen to the first movement of Vivaldi's *Gloria*. It lasts two and a
half minutes. Perhaps listen to it more than once. Simply allow its
beauty to enter your heart.

A Biblical Way of Praying the Mass

In the fifteenth century, Fra Angelico painted the Fiesole Altarpiece in the Church of San Domenico, near Florence. The predella (lower panel) comprises five smaller, horizontally placed paintings. The central panel shows Christ glorified in the court of heaven. A golden light radiates from him. Around him, angels sing and play musical instruments.

In the panel to the left we see ranks of saints facing the risen Christ. Mary kneels at the head of the uppermost row, her hands composed in prayer. Saint Peter stands beside her holding a book and the keys of the kingdom of heaven. Saint Dominic, too, appears in this upper row.

To the right, Fra Angelico depicts biblical figures and men and women martyrs. These, too, face Christ. Among them are Saint John the Baptist, Saint Stephen, and Saint Thecla. The two outermost panels, one to the left and the other to the right, portray Dominican figures of holiness, men and women in their black and white habits. In the panel to the right, gazing at Christ, Saint Catherine of Siena kneels at the head of the women.

To my mind, few painters equal Fra Angelico in the visual representation of holiness. The serene, joyful majesty of the figures and the beauty of the colors awaken in the viewer a sense of the sacred. In these panels, the peace, love, warmth, and serene happiness of the angels and the blessed in heaven lift the observer's heart. What Vivaldi does audibly, Fra Angelico does visually: the viewer glimpses the love and joy that flow between Christ and the heavenly court.

An Internet search for "Fra Angelico Fiesole altarpiece" will find the three central panels of this predella. I invite you to look at it. Enlarge it. View the ranks of angels and contemplate several of them individually. Examine the saints and how Fra Angelico painted them. Allow a sense of the heavenly host to rise in your heart.

C. S. Lewis's novel *That Hideous Strength* is both a grim portrayal of evil and a beautiful story of conversion. At one point, Jane, who has no life of faith, meets Ransom, whom she knows as the Director.[47] In that meeting, her godless world is undone. As they conclude their conversation, a simple meal is brought to the Director. He eats, tips the remaining crumbs to the floor, and blows a single note on a small whistle. Three small mice approach, and Jane, to her surprise, is not repelled. With rapid movements, they consume the crumbs and return whence they came. The Director smiles and tells Jane that this simple procedure satisfies all: humans do not want crumbs, and mice are happy to have them.

Jane, somewhat unexpectedly, finds herself considering how huge human beings must seem to the mice. Then she realizes that she is experiencing not her own hugeness with respect to the mice but rather a hugeness outside of herself that has drawn near. The Director recognizes the approach of an angel—in the novel, an *eldil*—and, knowing that Jane is not prepared for this, gently prompts her to exit the room.

Now Jane is on the train returning home. Many things stir in her heart as she recalls her meeting with the Director. Her worldview has changed. One part of her protests, but another part welcomes this new understanding. Above all, however, Jane is simply and supremely happy, filled with life and radiant.

God now begins to be real for Jane, and she has experienced the approach of an angel. She is changed, and a joy she has never known

---

[47] C. S. Lewis, *That Hideous Strength*, chap. 7.

expands in her heart. Lewis's narrative, in its different way, also permits a glimpse of heavenly glory, of angelic majesty, and of ineffable joy.

But the most complete view of the heavenly court as it sings God's praises is found in Scripture. John is shown a vision of "a great multitude, which no one could count, from every nation, race, people, and tongue." They stand "before the throne and before the Lamb, wearing white robes and holding palm branches in their hands" (Rev. 7:9). Their hearts thrill with the joy of salvation, of victory won through the blood of the Lamb, and for the gift of eternal life. In loud voices, they cry out, "Salvation comes from our God, who is seated on the throne, and from the Lamb" (Rev. 7:10).

The angels, the elders, and the four living creatures prostrate themselves before the throne, worship God, and exclaim, "Amen. Blessing and glory, wisdom and thanksgiving, honor, power, and might be to our God forever and ever. Amen" (Rev. 7:12). They give glory to God, their hearts filled with gratitude and their voices lifted in praise. Can we visualize this scene as John describes it? Can we grasp what these words express? Mindful of those who so joyfully proclaim them, I invite you to say each of these words slowly, allowing its meaning to enter your heart:

> Salvation,
> blessing,
> glory,
> wisdom,
> thanksgiving,
> honor,
> power,
> and might
> be to our God.

∽

Venerable Bruno writes, "At the Preface, I will seek the sentiments and the heart of the Heavenly Court." In the later version, with slightly different words, he invites us to seek "the sentiments of the Blessed in heaven."

The conclusion of the Preface reads as follows:

> And so, with Angels and Archangels,
> with Thrones and Dominions,
> and with all the hosts and Powers of heaven,
> we sing the hymn of your glory,
> as without end we acclaim:
> Holy, Holy, Holy Lord God of hosts ...[48]

We proclaim God's holiness "with Angels and Archangels, with Thrones and Dominions, and with all the hosts and Powers of heaven." When we pray, "Holy, Holy, Holy Lord God of hosts. Heaven and earth are full of your glory," we say this prayer *together with the Heavenly Court.* Joined with them in praise, Venerable Bruno invites us to pray these words with their same sentiments and heart, with deep gratitude for God's saving love, with hearts raised in thanksgiving and adoration, and with the joy of those who sing the heavenly song.

Have you ever considered that, when the priest prays the Preface, when you join your heart to his words as you listen, and when you say or sing the Holy, Holy, Holy, you are praying with the angels, the archangels, and all the heavenly host? Stop briefly now and consider this truth.

---

[48] Preface I of the Sundays in Ordinary Time.

A Biblical Way of Praying the Mass

∞

Contemplate the Heavenly Court for a moment (see image 7). "See" and "hear" the angels and the blessed gathered around the throne as they worship, adore, and sing God's praises with glad hearts. Let the warm and joyful sentiments of their hearts fill your own heart.

Then, with this heart, slowly pray the following Preface.[49] The following text gives the Preface with its introductory dialogue and the Holy, Holy, Holy that concludes it:

The Lord be with you.

And with your spirit.

Lift up your hearts (yes, lift up your heart in praise).

We lift them up to the Lord.

Let us give thanks to the Lord our God (thanks for so many blessings received).

It is right and just.

It is truly right and just, our duty and our salvation (to give thanks to God is truly right, truly just, a duty, and a means of salvation),

always and everywhere to give you thanks (always, everywhere),

Lord, holy Father, almighty and eternal God, through Christ our Lord.

For through his Paschal Mystery (his death and Resurrection),

---

[49] Preface I of the Sundays in Ordinary Time.

he accomplished the marvelous deed, by which he has freed us from the yoke of sin and death (free, in him, to live without sin, free for life beyond death),

summoning us to the glory of being now called

a chosen race, a royal priesthood (we are this race and this priesthood),

a holy nation, a people for your own possession (and a holy nation, belonging to the One who loves us),

to proclaim everywhere your mighty works (proclaim these by our lives, our witness, our words),

for you have called us out of darkness into your own wonderful light (you have given us Christ as our light and guide in this life).

And so, with Angels and Archangels,

with Thrones and Dominions,

and with all the hosts and Powers of heaven (united with the Heavenly Court),

we sing the hymn of your glory,

as without end we acclaim:

Holy, Holy, Holy Lord God of hosts.

Heaven and earth are full of your glory (the vision of Isaiah: "Holy, holy, holy, is the LORD of Hosts! All the earth is filled with his glory!" [Isa. 6:3]).

Hosanna in the highest (hosanna: a cry of praise and adoration).

A Biblical Way of Praying the Mass

Blessed is he who comes in the name of the Lord (the crowds call to Jesus on Palm Sunday, "Hosanna! Blessed is he who comes in the name of the Lord!" [Mark 11:9]).

Hosanna in the highest.

Pray the Preface and the Holy, Holy, Holy this way when you are at Mass, with these sentiments and with this heart.

12

Jesus's Heart

Now I want to become different, to be wholly
Christian, with all that that word means of
forgetfulness of self, strength, serenity, and love.

— Servant of God Elisabeth Leseur

The Preface has introduced the Eucharistic Prayer, "the heart and summit of the celebration" (CCC 1352). Now, acting in the person of Christ, the priest takes the bread in his hands and says, "Take this, all of you, and eat of it, for this is my Body, which will be given up for you." Then, over the chalice, "Take this all of you, and drink from it, for this is the chalice of my Blood."

In this "summit of the celebration," what fills our hearts? What stirs within? Venerable Bruno writes, "At the Consecration, I will seek the sentiments and the heart of Christ."

Let your heart be stilled. Let it reach the deep point. Let an awareness of Jesus's self-offering arise in your heart. Unite your heart with Jesus's, offering with him your life, yourself, to the Father.

∞

In retrospect, I recognize that my pastor Father James Woulfe saw in me a future priest. Through my high school years, he fostered that vocation in unobtrusive ways, and I remain grateful. Occasionally, he gave me books to read. One day, he gave me *To Know Christ Jesus* by Frank Sheed, published a few years earlier. It was the best book he could have chosen.

It opened a new world for me. The title is from Saint Paul's words, "I even consider everything as a loss because of the supreme good of knowing Christ Jesus my Lord" (Phil. 3:8). I marveled at the author's knowledge of Scripture and his ability to cite relevant passages. I did not know that Scripture could be explored in this way to learn about Jesus.

To know Christ Jesus: yes, that is the supreme good, and the more we know his Heart, the more we can live the Consecration when at Mass. "At the Consecration, I will seek the sentiments and the heart of Christ."

What were the sentiments and what filled the Heart of Christ when he offered himself to the Father for us? Scripture is our best guide here. I invite you to read the following texts slowly. Allow the words to enter your heart and to reveal to you the Heart of Jesus.

> **"This is my body.... This is my blood of the covenant, which will be shed on behalf of many for the forgiveness of sins"** (Matt. 26:26–28): a Heart that offers everything, even his Body, even his Blood—all that he is—that our sins may be forgiven and the door to eternal life opened.

> **"I am the good shepherd. A good shepherd lays down his life for the sheep"** (John 10:11): again, a Heart that offers itself without limit, laying down his life for his sheep—for us.

> **"He loved his own in the world and he loved them to the end"** (John 13:1): a Heart that loves without measure, to

the end—that is, to the last moment of his life and to the utmost bounds of love.

"He emptied himself, taking the form of a slave" (Phil. 2:7): a Heart that gives its whole being, totally available to the Father in our service and for our liberation.

"Father, if it is possible, let this cup pass from me; yet, not as I will, but as you will" (Matt. 26:39): a Heart in agony, a human Heart that struggles to say yes to the Father and that offers itself without reserve.

Can you ask for the sentiments and the Heart of Christ as you live the Consecration in the Mass? Could there be a richer and more fruitful way to experience this moment?

Throughout his pontificate, Saint John Paul II referred repeatedly to what he called the "Law of the Gift." He cited the teaching of Vatican II that the human person "cannot fully find himself except through the sincere gift of himself."[50] The council refers to Jesus's teaching that "whoever seeks to preserve his life will lose it, but whoever loses it will save it" (Luke 17:33). Saint John Paul II comments, "In this way, Jesus proclaims that life finds its center, its meaning, and its fulfillment when it is given up."[51]

We cannot fully find ourselves—that is, become fully what God intended us to be, live life in the richest measure, find a deeply satisfying happiness—*except through the sincere gift of ourselves* in

---

[50] Second Vatican Council, Pastoral Constitution on the Church in the Modern World *Gaudium et spes* (December 7, 1965), no. 24, author's translation.

[51] Pope Saint John Paul II, Encyclical *Evangelium Vitae* (*The Gospel of Life*) (March 25, 1995), no. 51.

A Biblical Way of Praying the Mass

love to God and to those he has placed in our lives. Saint John Paul II understood this truth as fundamental in our lives. The Law of the Gift is the only path to personal fulfillment and to joy in this life and the next. The Consecration in the Mass is the supreme instance of this law and the primary source of the grace that helps us live it. When we ask for a heart like Christ's, we are asking to live the Law of the Gift.

In one of his talks, Venerable Fulton Sheen shared a story that I never forgot. A young girl was sitting in the kitchen of her home, watching her mother as she worked. This day, she asked a question she had long wanted to raise. Her mother's hands were covered with scars. With the bluntness of a child, the girl said, "Mother, how did your hands get so ugly?" Her mother replied, "When you were a baby, one day you were sleeping upstairs in your crib. While you slept, the house caught fire. I ran upstairs and found that your blankets had already caught the flames. I tore the blankets off from you, picked you up, and ran with you out of the house. That is how I got these scars." The young girl looked at her mother and said, "Mother, I love your scars."

I love your scars. Nothing is happier in this life than to hear on the lips of another, or to read in the eyes of another, these words: "I love your scars." I love the way you have given of yourself for me, the way you have given me your time, your listening ear, your help, how you were there for me when I needed you, even when it cost you tiredness and sacrifice. *I love your scars.* We cannot, Saint John Paul II tells us, fully find ourselves except through the sincere gift of ourselves.

Chiara Lejeune, daughter of the Servant of God Jérôme Lejeune, doctor and geneticist, recounts a conversation with her father in his last moments: "He spoke in short gasps, stopping from time to time to breathe some oxygen.... I asked him if he wanted to bequeath something to his little patients [young children]. He answered,

'No, I don't mean to neglect them, but, you see, I don't own very much. Besides, I gave them my whole life, and my life was all I had.' "[52] Again, we cannot fully find ourselves except through the sincere gift of ourselves.

A ten-minute walk from our rectory is the barbershop where I go for haircuts. One day, a new barber was there, a frail woman in her late sixties. As she cut, we began talking. She was a woman of faith, active in her church. She told me of her heart condition and her anxiety about the medical treatment involved. I had recently published a book on overcoming spiritual discouragement and asked if she would like a copy. She replied with an energetic yes.

The following days were busy, and each day I looked at the book and decided, a little shamefacedly, that I did not have time to walk the ten minutes to give it her. Ten days after the haircut, I did. When she saw that I had brought the book, her eyes brightened. She clasped my hand and thanked me again and again. It was the warmest and most uplifting moment of the day. I thought to myself, "Why did I wait ten days?" Such experiences show me what the Law of the Gift means in daily living.

Saint John of the Cross writes, "All good things were given to me when I no longer sought them through self-love."[53] Saint Thérèse of Lisieux cites these words and reflects that those who most love God and others are themselves most loved. She writes, "We seek their company; we render them services without their asking; finally, these souls so capable of bearing with the lack of respect and consideration of others see themselves surrounded with everyone's affection. We may apply to them these words of

[52] Chiara Lejeune, *Life Is a Blessing: A Biography of Jérôme Lejeune — Geneticist, Doctor, Father* (San Francisco: Ignatius Press, 2000), 135.

[53] Kieran Kavanaugh, OCD, ed. and trans., *The Collected Works of Saint John of the Cross* (Washington, DC: ICS Publications, 1991), 110–111. These words are found in John's *Sketch of Mount Carmel*.

our Father St. John of the Cross: 'All good things were given to me when I no longer sought them through self-love.' "[54]

On August 15, 2000, I watched on television as Saint John Paul II met with three hundred thousand young people in the square outside St. John Lateran's church in Rome. It was the opening ceremony of World Youth Day. A larger crowd awaited him in Saint Peter's Square. The double ceremony was necessary to accommodate the great numbers present. The pope began his scripted talk. When he quoted his often-repeated words "Do not be afraid! Open, open wide the doors to Christ!" the crowd of young people applauded and chanted, "Viva il Papa!" and "John Paul II, we love you!" A tremendous outpouring of love and affection rose from them to the pope. When they would not stop, the pope surrendered. He set the text of his talk on his knee, placed his hand on the side of his head, and, deeply moved, smiled and interacted with them. He never finished his talk.

As I watched, I found myself deeply stirred as well. I said to myself: I am seeing the Law of the Gift before my eyes. For twenty-one years, this eighty-year-old man has spent himself in teaching, traveling, preaching, writing, and events like this, for the Church and for these young people. They know that he loves them and has given himself for them. And now, a powerful wave of love envelops him in return. Yes, we cannot fully find ourselves except through the sincere gift of ourselves.

In the Consecration of the Mass, the priest pronounces the words of Christ: "This is my Body, which will be given up for you," and "This is the chalice of my Blood ... which will be poured out for you." Jesus gives himself totally — *even his Body and his Blood* — out

---

[54] *Story of a Soul: The Autobiography of Saint Thérèse of Lisieux*, trans. John Clarke, OCD (Washington, DC: ICS Publications, 1996), 245–246. I have translated "*tous les biens*" as "all good things" rather than "all goods," as in the translation I have quoted here.

of love for us (see image 8). When Venerable Bruno calls us to live the Consecration with the heart and sentiments of Jesus, he invites us to embrace the Law of the Gift in our lives—the most demanding and the happiest invitation we will ever receive. In Jesus's self-gift, we find not only a model to imitate but also the strength we need to live this law.

"At the Consecration, I will seek the sentiments and the heart of Christ." Take a moment now to reread the following Gospel verses. Do not hurry through them. Allow them to speak to your heart and reveal to you the sentiments and the Heart of Christ in his self-offering of love for you.

> **"This is my body.... This is my blood of the covenant, which will be shed on behalf of many for the forgiveness of sins"** (Matt. 26:26–28). What fills Jesus's Heart as he says these words?

> **"I am the good shepherd. A good shepherd lays down his life for the sheep"** (John 10:11). What sentiments stir in Jesus's Heart when he pronounces these words and declares his willingness to lay down his life for his sheep—for us?

> **"He loved his own in the world and he loved them to the end"** (John 13:1). *To the end:* What love do these words express?

> **"He emptied himself, taking the form of a slave"** (Phil. 2:7). What does Jesus's self-emptying mean? What does his Heart experience as he empties himself out of love for us?

> **"Father, if it is possible, let this cup pass from me; yet, not as I will, but as you will"** (Matt. 26:39). What willingness

to love and what degree of love are expressed in this embrace of his Father's will?

Now, aware of the "sentiments and heart of Christ" in his self-giving, read, ponder, meditate, and unhurriedly pray the words of the Consecration at Mass. You may find it fruitful to do so more than once and on more than one day. Such meditation will help you to live the Consecration with the sentiments and heart of Christ.

On the day before he was to suffer (Holy Thursday evening, in the upper room),

he took bread in his holy and venerable hands (in your mind's eye, contemplate Jesus as he does this and the following actions),

and with eyes raised to heaven,

to you, O God, his almighty Father,

giving you thanks, he said the blessing,

broke the bread,

and gave it to his disciples, saying:

Take this, all of you, and eat of it ("take," "eat": the Law of the Gift),

for this is my Body,

which will be given up for you ("my Body," "given up for you").

In a similar way, when supper was ended,

he took this precious chalice

in his holy and venerable hands (again, contemplate Jesus as he does this and the following actions),

and once more giving you thanks, he said the blessing and gave the chalice to his disciples, saying:

Take this, all of you, and drink from it,

for this is the chalice of my Blood,

the Blood of the new and eternal covenant,

which will be poured out for you and for many ("my Blood," "poured out for you": the Law of the Gift)

for the forgiveness of sins.

Do this in memory of me (in the Consecration of the Mass, the Church fulfills this blessed command; in it we find the model and the grace to live by it).

Ask for a heart that prays the Consecration of the Mass with these sentiments.

13

Give Us This Day

Our Father who art in heaven, see before
you one of your sons, who places himself in
your hands, and gives you his heart.

— Venerable Bruno Lanteri

Some years ago, I worked with a group that emphasized our relationship with God as Father. This was not new, but the repeated reference to God as Father and the invitation to relate to God as Father led to something new in my prayer. When Jesus is baptized, the Father proclaims, "You are my beloved Son; with you I am well pleased" (Mark 1:11), a verse this group often cited. Through Baptism, we are made adopted sons in Jesus, and that Father's love is bestowed upon us as well. We, too, receive these words from the Father, "You are my beloved son, my beloved daughter." I realized that to relate to God as Father is to know that I am loved, that I am beloved in his heart.

This awareness deepened as time passed. Other scriptural verses added their richness. In the Old Testament I read, "When Israel was a child I loved him.... It was I who taught Ephraim to walk, who took them in my arms.... I drew them with human cords, with bands of love; I fostered them like those who raise an infant to their cheeks; I bent down to feed them" (Hos. 11:1, 3–4).

Jesus tells us, "As the Father loves me, so I also love you" (John 15:9) — that is, in the way the Father loves Jesus, he, Jesus, loves us. Jesus prays to his Father for the unity of his disciples so that the world may know "that you loved them even as you loved me" (John 17:23). Even brief reflection on these words plunges us into the depths of the Father's love for us: he loves us *even as he loves Jesus*. Paul tells us that we received "a spirit of adoption, through which we cry, 'Abba, Father!'" (Rom. 8:15), with all the closeness this word "Abba" entails.

A few years ago, I spent eighteen months reading the writings of Saint Thérèse of Lisieux and many books about her. I found this deeper acquaintance with her nourishing and uplifting. I understood why Thérèse instinctively knew that the image of God as severe and ready to condemn could not be right: her experience of her own father, Saint Louis Martin, was radically different. One quote from *The Story of a Soul* will suffice. Thérèse recalls the evenings at home in her childhood:

> What shall I say of the winter evenings at home, especially the Sunday evenings? Ah! how I loved, after the *game of checkers* was over, to sit with Céline on Papa's knees. He used to sing, in his beautiful voice, airs that filled the soul with profound thoughts, or else, rocking us gently, he recited poems that taught the eternal truths. Then we all went upstairs to say our night prayers together and the little Queen was alone near her King, having only to look at him to see how the saints pray. When prayer was ended we came according to age to bid Papa good night and receive his kiss; the *Queen* naturally came last and the *King* took her by the two elbows to kiss her and she could cry out in a high-pitched

tone: "Good night, Papa, good night and sleep well!" Every evening was a repetition of the same thing.[55]

For Thérèse, if God was our Father, he was above all love.

In his own life, Venerable Bruno experienced the love of his father, Pietro, and the selfless dedication of his spiritual father, Father Nikolaus von Diessbach. Bruno's experience, too, of fatherhood was enveloped in goodness and love.[56]

At this point in the Mass, we turn to our heavenly Father and pray to him with the words Jesus gave us. Venerable Bruno writes, "At the Our Father, I will seek the sentiments and the heart of one who asks for what he needs."

I have translated Venerable Bruno's single word *mendico* as "one who asks for what he needs." *Mendico* is defined as "a person in need, reduced to extreme poverty, who must beg in order to survive."[57] The word applies when our need is great, when we are unable to meet it on our own, and we turn to one who can supply what we need, asking for this help with all our heart.

Biblical examples of hearts like this abound. In a time of imminent danger, Esther prays, "My Lord, you alone are our King. Help me, who am alone and have no help but you" (Esther 4:14). When the people suffer and all human support is removed, Daniel implores, "Now, our God, hear the prayer and petition of your servant; and for your own sake, Lord, let your face shine upon your

---

[55] *Story of a Soul*, 43.

[56] See Timothy M. Gallagher, OMV, *Overcoming Spiritual Discouragement: The Wisdom and Spiritual Power of Venerable Bruno Lanteri* (Irondale, AL: EWTN Publishing, 2019), 16–17.

[57] *Dizionario di Italiano*, s.v. "mendico," author's translation, https://dizionari.corriere.it/dizionario_italiano/M/mendico.shtml.

desolate sanctuary.... Lord, be attentive and act without delay, for your own sake, my God, because your name is invoked upon your city and your people!" (Dan. 9:17, 19).

The leper, helpless in every way, kneels before Jesus and cries from his heart, "If you wish, you can make me clean" (Mark 1:40). Jairus pleads, "My daughter is at the point of death. Please, come and lay your hands on her that she may get well and live" (Mark 5:23). The centurion appeals to Jesus saying, "Lord, my servant is lying at home paralyzed, suffering dreadfully" (Matt. 8:6). In these and many other instances in Scripture, such visceral, heartfelt prayers, born of pressing need and made with great trust, are heard. Venerable Bruno invites us to pray the Our Father at Mass with similar hearts and sentiments.

The heart of a *mendico* is richly expressed in the first beatitude: "Blessed are the poor in spirit, for theirs is the kingdom of heaven" (Matt. 5:3). Blessed are those who know their own insufficiency, who know that they need God, that they need his help, and ask for it with confidence in the loving Father to whom they turn.

In Alessandro Manzoni's classic novel *The Betrothed*, Renzo, a main character, faces a time of urgent need. He finds himself near a chapel and approaches it. Once there, he prays:

> On reaching the foot of the chapel, he went and knelt down on the bottom step, and there offered up to God a prayer, or rather a medley of broken phrases, exclamation, entreaties, promises, and laments—one of those addresses that are never made to other men, for others have not enough penetration to understand them or patience to listen to them.[58]

---

[58] Alessandro Manzoni, *The Betrothed*, trans. A. Colquhoun (New York: E. P. Dutton, 1961), 561.

These are the sentiments, and this is the heart of a *mendico*. Renzo's prayer is heard.

In the spiritual classic *The Cloud of Unknowing*, the author's illustration of the prayer of the heart may apply here as well:

> Let me try to illustrate what I mean with an example from real life. A man or woman terrified by sudden disaster is forced by the circumstances to the limits of his personal resources, and marshals all his energy into one great cry for help. In extreme situations like this, a person is not given to many words nor even to long ones. Instead, summoning all his strength, he expresses his desperate need in one loud cry: "Help!" And with this one little word he effectively arouses the attention and assistance of others.... And so this simple prayer bursting from the depth of your spirit touches the heart of Almighty God.[59]

The author references the biblical teaching that such prayer "pierces the heavens" (see Sir. 35:17, RSVCE). This, too, is the prayer of the *mendico*.

Years ago, a Catholic doctor cited the prayer of the thief on the cross (Luke 23:42) and told me, "My prayer is very simple, 'Jesus, remember me when you come into your kingdom.' It's all there. God's redeeming love is always happening. It's happening now. That is my whole prayer." I have never forgotten the doctor's words, and their meaning deepens as time passes. "Jesus, remember me." This prayer is a cry of utter helplessness and need brought with faith to Jesus. We know the lovely sequel, "*Today* you will be with me." At times, it seems to me as well that this

---

[59] William Johnston, ed., *The Cloud of Unknowing and The Book of Privy Counseling: An Enduring Classic of Christian Mystical Experience* (Garden City, NY: Image Books, 1973), 95–96.

prayer is the summary of all our prayer. Venerable Bruno invites us to pray the Our Father at Mass with a similar awareness of our need and with confidence that Jesus welcomes and lovingly answers our prayer.

How can we grow toward praying the Our Father in this way? Saint Ignatius of Loyola proposes a simple and profound method. He invites us to pray the Our Father unhurriedly, word by word, in the following manner: "Let the person say 'Father,' and stay with this word as long as he finds meanings, comparisons, relish, and consolation in considerations relating to this word, and let him do likewise with each word of the Our Father."[60]

During my seminary years, this was proposed to us as a form of prayer available in any circumstance: on hectic days when finding material for prayer would be otherwise difficult, during a long drive, in free moments, while walking, when exercising, and so forth. Here was a text always at our fingertips, with words given by Jesus himself, inexhaustibly rich—a prayer, as Saint Cyprian wrote, "overflowing with spiritual strength," and a "summary of heavenly teaching" in which "nothing is omitted that may be found in our prayers and petition."[61]

Consider praying the Our Father in this way outside of Mass and perhaps more than once. If you do, the words will acquire deeper meaning. Then you will more readily pray the Our Father at Mass in the way Venerable Bruno proposes.

---

[60] *Spiritual Exercises*, 252, author's translation. Saint Ignatius adds that the Hail Mary and other prayers may also be meditated on in this way.

[61] Saint Cyprian, *De Dominica Oratione*, in Corpus Christianorum, Series Latina 3A (Turnholti: Typographi Brepols Editores Pontificii, 1976), 94, author's translation.

∞

Take time now, if you can, to pray the Our Father. Remain with each word or set of words "as long as you find meanings, comparisons, relish, and consolation" in praying with them. If you do not complete the prayer in one sitting, resume it another time.

Our Father: *Father*: ponder the love, the security, and the providential care of the heavenly Father that this word signifies. *Our*: all of us share this Father; we are all his sons and daughters, one family.

who art in heaven: lift your gaze of faith to the infinite joy of heaven where this Father resides with the Son and Holy Spirit, the communion to which we are called when earthly life is done.

hallowed be thy name: ask, beg, petition that this Father's name be held in love and reverence in your heart, in your family, in the Church, and in the world.

thy kingdom come: pray that the kingdom of God—his love, truth, life, holiness, grace, justice, and peace—grow and be increasingly rooted in this world. Desire this. Ask for this.

thy will be done: with the sentiments and heart of a *mendico*, seek the grace to do God's will in your life, in all things, day by day.

on earth: pray that God's will be done in the Church and in the world. Raise this cry from your heart.

as it is in heaven: contemplate the joy, the harmony, the communion, the peace of heaven, in which God's will is the single guide. Ask that this joy and communion be granted to our world.

A Biblical Way of Praying the Mass

Give us this day: What are your needs this day? What do your family members need this day? The Church? The nation? The world? Ask to be given what you need today.

our daily bread: the material bread we need for our lives and for the sustenance, health, education, and well-being of those entrusted to our care; and the spiritual bread: the Eucharist, Holy Communion.

and forgive us our trespasses: ask for the loving encounter with the Father that is forgiveness (Luke 15:11–32), for healing from the burdens of our hearts.

as we forgive those who trespass against us: Has anyone hurt you? Mistreated you? Misunderstood you? In these deep places of the heart, ask for the grace to forgive. "Be kind to one another, compassionate, forgiving one another as God has forgiven you in Christ" (Eph. 4:32).

and lead us not into temptation: pray for freedom from all that could cause spiritual harm. Make this prayer for yourself, your family, the Church, and the world.

but deliver us from evil: ask for protection and safety from all evil. Ask this "of him who called you out of darkness into his wonderful light" (1 Pet. 2:9).

14

The Lamb and Mercy

*If I should fall a thousand times a day, a
thousand times a day I will begin again.*

—Venerable Bruno Lanteri

Twelve years after ordination, I was named provincial of the United
States province of my religious community. I served in this role
for ten years.

The beginnings entailed a steep learning curve as I dealt with
new financial, legal, and spiritual responsibilities. Through it all,
one thing gave me peace: whatever wisdom I had yet to acquire, I
knew that I was doing my best to serve the province.

Then a time came when that peace was shaken. A significant
opportunity for new and fruitful ministry arose. We lost it. Human
differences, frustrations, and lack of communication were involved,
and I was not without fault.

With this burden in my heart, I spoke with my spiritual director.
His reply helped me, and I wrote his words in my journal: "This
is what mercy is, when we are at fault, and there are real conse-
quences. Then God touches this situation. We sincerely express
our sorrow, and he forgives us, and that is that: it's over. And he

can give us something better than what was lost. He can bring good out of the troubled situation."

Before the year ended, I saw the truth of his words. The door to that opportunity reopened, and this time things were different. The communication involved was both demanding and healing. It proved a turning point that blessed the remainder of my time as provincial. The new ministry flourished, and relational bonds were stronger than before.

I remember that experience when I contemplate God's mercy: the wonderful confidence that when we bring our sinfulness and failings to him, God not only heals our wounds but will give something better than would have happened had we never failed.

I return often to one sentence in Saint John Paul II's letter on the mercy of God, *Dives in Misericordia*: "The true and proper meaning of mercy does not consist only in looking, however penetratingly and compassionately, at moral, physical, or material evil: mercy is manifested in its true and proper aspect when it restores to value, promotes and draws good from all the forms of evil existing in the world and in man."[62] It is a true "John Paul II" sentence, dense with meaning. A phrase-by-phrase review of it will best help us absorb its content.

The true and proper meaning of mercy (its fullest meaning)

does not consist only in looking (noticing, seeing, not missing),

however penetratingly and compassionately (with a clear perception of the other's situation, received with a warm and loving heart),

---

[62] Pope Saint John Paul II, Encyclical on the Mercy of God *Dives in Misericordia* (November 30, 1980), no. 6.

at moral (sin and all its ravages),

physical (hunger, disease, death),

or material evil (poverty, lack of shelter, suffering from various disasters):

Comment: This understanding of mercy is already great! When we encounter moral, physical, or material evil and our hearts are moved; when we do not pass by but perceive and turn toward this pain with compassion, we are well on the road to mercy. Blessed as this response to suffering is, however, it is not yet the "true and proper meaning" of mercy.

mercy is manifested in its true and proper aspect (in its fullest meaning)

when it restores to value (undoes the harm of evil, gives back what was lost),

promotes (fosters healing and growth where suffering and evil reigned)

and draws good (we bring our wounds to God, and he *draws good* out of our failures, even out of our sinfulness)

from all the forms of evil existing in the world and in man (no evil of any kind, in any person, or anywhere in the world is excluded from God's mercy when we turn to him).

Comment: As I contemplate this sentence, I understand anew why Saint John Paul II could repeat so often, "Do not be afraid!" To know that mercy, with this rich meaning, is always available to us removes the burdens we may carry as we view our lives: there is *nothing*—no moral, physical, or material evil—that God cannot use for good when we open our hearts to his mercy.

A Biblical Way of Praying the Mass

Venerable Bruno writes, "At the Lamb of God, I will seek the sentiments and the heart of one who is guilty and in need of forgiveness."
I have translated Venerable Bruno's single word *reo* as "one who is
guilty and in need of forgiveness." More literally, a *reo* is one who
has "committed an act or behaved in a way that is against the law
and is subject to a legal penalty."[63] Transferred to the spiritual realm,
a *reo* is one who knows that he or she has acted contrary to Jesus's
teaching—through self-centeredness, impatience, lack of charity,
anger, or through any of the seven capital sins and their unhappy
expressions in act—and brings this awareness to Jesus, the Lamb
of God, seeking that wonderful gift of mercy just described. When,
Venerable Bruno says, you pray the threefold invocation, "Lamb
of God, you take away the sins of the world, have mercy on us ...
have mercy on us ... grant us peace," pray it with these sentiments
and with this heart.

Biblical examples of such prayer abound. The classic expression of
a *reo* who turns to God and begs from his heart for healing mercy
is David in Psalm 51, presented as his prayer after his sin. It may
help at this point to take the Bible and pray Psalm 51 in its entirety.
Its content will bless your praying of the Lamb of God at Mass. A
few verses will reveal why:

> **Have mercy on me, God, in accord with your merciful
> love** (I turn to you and to the merciful love that I know
> fills your heart);
>
> **in your abundant compassion blot out my transgres-
> sions** (blot out: remove thoroughly)....

[63] *Dizionario di Italiano*, s.v. "reo," author's translation, https://dizionari.
corriere.it/dizionario_italiano/R/reato.shtml..

Cleanse me with hyssop, that I may be pure (make me clean; make me pure);

wash me, and I will be whiter than snow (spiritually "whiter than snow"!).

You will let me hear gladness and joy (joy in place of my heaviness of heart)....

My sacrifice, O God, is a contrite spirit (a contrite spirit: the sincere, humble heart of a *reo*, which draws upon it God's mercy);

A contrite, humbled heart, O God, you will not scorn (our God receives such prayer from such hearts). (Ps. 51:3, 9–10, 19)

A further expression of of a *reo*'s prayer is Psalm 130, much loved by Saint Alphonsus Liguori. I once visited a parish staffed by his Redemptorist priests. On the altar were engraved the words of this psalm, "*Copiosa apud eum redemptio,*" "With him is plenteous redemption" (v. 7). Each time I approached the altar for Mass, I saw these heartening words. In Psalm 130 we pray:

Out of the depths I call to you, LORD (from that place of burden in my heart);

LORD, hear my cry!

May your ears be attentive

to my cry for mercy (Lord, hear the cry of my heart, my prayer for mercy!).

If you, LORD, keep account of sins,

LORD, who can stand? (you know our fragility; you are not a harsh judge; you love the humanity you created)....

A Biblical Way of Praying the Mass

Let Israel hope in the LORD,

For with the LORD is mercy,

with him is plenteous redemption (plenteous, abundant, overflowing mercy, redemption, healing). (Ps. 130:1–3, 7)

What if we prayed to the Lamb of God at Mass with sentiments like these?

A third scriptural illustration will suffice. The people have turned from God, and a time of great suffering follows. Daniel fasts and clothes himself in sackcloth and ashes. He prays from his heart:

> Now, our God, hear the prayer and petition of your servant; and for your own sake, Lord, let your face shine upon your desolate sanctuary.
>
> Give ear, my God, and listen; open your eyes and look upon our desolate city upon which your name is invoked. When we present our petition before you, we rely not on our just deeds, but on your great mercy.
>
> Lord, hear! Lord, pardon! Lord, be attentive and act without delay, for your own sake, my God, because your name is invoked upon your city and your people! (Dan. 9:17–19).

Lord, hear! Lord, pardon! When you pray to the Lamb of God at Mass, Venerable Bruno says, ask for a heart like Daniel's.

Turn now to Jesus. The Baptist sees him and proclaims, "Behold, the Lamb of God, who takes away the sin of the world" (John 1:29). His words evoke the prophecy of Isaiah, "Though harshly treated, he submitted/ and did not open his mouth;/ Like a lamb led to the slaughter/ or a sheep silent before shearers,/ he did not open his mouth" (Isa. 53:7). In heaven, the angels, the living creatures, and the elders cry out with loud voices, "Worthy is the Lamb that was slain to receive power and riches, wisdom and strength, honor and glory and blessing" (Rev. 5:12).

Open your heart now to Jesus, the Lamb of God (see image 9). Meditate briefly on the three parts of the prayer we say at Mass, and do so with the humble openness and great confidence of a *reo*:

Lamb of God (ponder the three Scriptures just cited),

You take away the sins of the world (*take away*, so that the burden is wholly, completely, utterly removed. "As far as the east is from the west, so far has he removed our sins from us" [Ps. 103:12]),

have mercy on us/grant us peace (reread the sentence of Saint John Paul II cited above. Slowly repeat Jesus's words: "Peace I leave with you; my peace I give to you. Not as the world gives do I give it to you. Do not let your hearts be troubled or afraid" [John 14:27]).

I sat before the television and watched the final Mass of World Youth Day in August of 2000. I listened as the frail, eighty-year-old John Paul II spoke to the millions of young people gathered before him. When he spoke the following words, a great applause arose from his listeners: "Yes, dear friends, Christ loves us, and he loves us forever! He loves us even when we disappoint him, when we fail to meet his expectations for us. He never fails to embrace us in his mercy. How can we not be grateful to this God who has redeemed us, going so far as to accept the foolishness of the Cross? To God who has come to be at our side and has stayed with us to the end?"[64]

---

[64] Homily of the Holy Father John Paul II for the closing of World Youth Day, Tor Vergata, August 20, 2000.

A Biblical Way of Praying the Mass

Yes, certainly they applauded! Such truths lift our hearts as well. Venerable Bruno invites us to turn to the Lamb of God at Mass knowing that "he never fails to embrace us in his mercy."

15

A Heart in Love

Love is sufficient of itself, it satisfies of itself and
because of itself. It is its own merit, its own reward.

—Saint Bernard of Clairvaux

On the morning of April 22, 1903, Elisabeth Leseur entered the
church of St. Peter's in Rome. Thirty-four years later, her cause
for canonization would be introduced, and she is today Servant of
God Elisabeth Leseur.

Remembering that day, she wrote:

I set out alone for St. Peter's, and after going to Confession to a French-speaking priest, I went to Communion in
the chapel of the Blessed Sacrament. Those moments were
completely and supernaturally happy.

I felt in myself the living presence of the blessed Christ,
of God Himself, bringing me an ineffable love; this incom-
parable Soul spoke to mine, and all the infinite tenderness
of the Savior passed for an instant into me. Never will this
divine trace be effaced. The triumphant Christ, the eternal
Word, He who as man has suffered and loved, the one living God, took possession of my soul for all eternity in that

unforgettable moment. I felt myself renewed to my very depths by Him, ready for a new life, for duty, for the work intended by His Providence. I gave myself without reserve, and I gave him the future.

I then heard Mass in another chapel, in profound joy and peace. I prayed again, and then I knelt close to the Confession, in a last intimate and solemn consecration.[65]

On December 3 of the following year, Elisabeth wrote of a confession that brought her peace, and continued:

Yesterday morning I went to Communion in the same peace and the same abandonment to God. I felt Christ Jesus truly living in me, and now I want to become different, to be wholly Christian, with all that that word means of forgetfulness of self, strength, serenity, and love.[66]

And two months later:

Yesterday I went to Communion with joy and renewed the offering of my life to Jesus my Savior. May He give me grace to be His apostle and to make known to souls, by my example and my deeds, the strength and life He gives to a soul and how He can transform a human being even as weak as I. The divine Spirit, who out of ignorant fishermen made Apostles of burning zeal, can make use of me to do a little good, and I fervently ask for this from Him.[67]

---

[65] Elisabeth Leseur, *My Spirit Rejoices: Diary of a Christian Soul in An Age of Unbelief* (Manchester, NH: Sophia Institute Press, 1996), 73–74. The "Confession" near which Elisabeth kneels is the semicircular space directly in front of Saint Peter's tomb.

[66] Ibid., 88.

[67] Ibid., 90.

A Heart in Love

On March 25, 1804, another Elizabeth walked to church. She was the thirty-year-old convert Elizabeth Seton, and she approached St. Peter's Church in Manhattan, where she would receive Communion for the first time. She described that March 25 in a letter to a friend:

> At last, Amabilia, at last GOD IS MINE AND I AM HIS! Now, let all go its round—*I Have Received Him.* The awful impressions of the evening before, fears of not having done all to prepare, and yet, even the transports of confidence and hope in His Goodness. MY GOD! To the last breath of life will I not remember this night of watching for morning dawn; the fearful beating heart so pressing to be gone; the long walk to town; but every step counted, nearer that street, then nearer that tabernacle, then nearer the moment He would enter the poor, poor little dwelling so all His own—and when He did, the first thought I remember was: "Let God arise, let His enemies be scattered!" [Ps. 68:2]—for it seemed to me my King had come to take His Throne, and instead of the humble, tender welcome I had expected to give Him, it was but a triumph of joy and gladness that the deliverer was come and my defense and shield and strength and salvation made mine for this world and the next.[68]

In her final years, Saint Thérèse of Lisieux , too, remembered her first Communion:

> Ah! How sweet was that first kiss of Jesus! It was a kiss of love; I felt that I was loved, and I said: "I love You, and I

---

[68] Joseph Dirvin, CM, *Mrs. Seton: Foundress of the American Sisters of Charity* (New York: Farrar, Strauss, 1962), 168–169.

give myself to You forever!" There were no demands made, no struggles, no sacrifices; for a long time now Jesus and poor little Thérèse looked at and understood each other. That day, it was no longer simply a look, it was a fusion; they were no longer two.[69]

Saint Thomas Aquinas writes:

O precious and wonderful banquet that brings us salvation and contains all sweetness! Could anything be of more intrinsic value? Under the old law it was the flesh of calves and goats that was offered, but here Christ himself, the true God, is set before us as our food. What could be more wonderful than this? No other sacrament has greater healing power; through it sins are purged away, virtues are increased, and the soul is enriched with an abundance of every spiritual gift.[70]

What dispositions of heart best prepare us to receive the Communion in which "Christ himself, the true God, is set before us as our food"? Venerable Bruno writes, "At Communion, I will seek the sentiments and the heart of one in love."

One in love.

Take a few minutes and slowly meditate on the following passages.

O God, you are my God —
it is you I seek! (let your heart feel this longing).

---

[69] *Story of a Soul*, 77.
[70] Quoted in *The Liturgy of the Hours*, 3:610.

For you my body yearns;
for you my soul thirsts (feel the deep desire of your
body-soul humanity for the One who alone can fully
satisfy). (Ps. 63:2)

"Come," says my heart, "seek his face";
your face, LORD, do I seek! (say these words, slowly,
unhurriedly, from your heart to Jesus). (Ps. 27:8)

Let Jesus now invite you to receive him in Communion. Ponder
his words. Let their meaning penetrate your heart and prepare you
for your next Communion:

I am the bread of life (John 6:48): What does it mean
that Jesus is the *bread* of your life?

My flesh is true food, and my blood is true drink (John
6:55): true food, true drink; the nourishment you need for
life in this world and the next.

Whoever eats my flesh and drinks my blood remains in
me and I in him (John 6:56): desire this, a lasting, ongo-
ing, abiding, union with Jesus. Ask for it now. Prepare to
receive it.

Then, hear Saint Anselm's call to prepare your heart for the Lord.
His words will help dispose you for Mass as a whole and more
specifically for Communion. Read them slowly, reflectively, prayer-
fully, and from your heart. Receive the invitation they express:

Come now, O little soul, escape from your everyday business for a short while, hide for a moment from your restless

thoughts. Break off from your cares and troubles and be less concerned about your tasks and labors. Make a little time for God and rest a while in him.

Enter into your mind's inner chamber. Shut out everything but God and whatever helps you to seek him; and when you have shut the door, look for him. Speak now to God and say with your whole heart: I seek your face; your face Lord I desire.[71]

---

[71] Saint Anselm, *Proslogion*, quoted in *The Liturgy of the Hours*, 1:184. I have translated the first three Latin words, *Eia nunc, homuncio*, as "Come now, O little soul." *Homuncio*, translated more literally, signifies "little man."

16

Sent to the World

Those assembled are sent forth to bring the
fruits of the Eucharist to the world.

—General Instruction of the Roman Missal

Earlier in these reflections, we noted that Saints Louis and Zélie Martin, the parents of Saint Thérèse, faithfully attended daily Mass. We may now ask: What impact did that morning Mass have on the rest of their day? Their love for each other and for their children, the faith-filled care with which they raised them, their mutual assistance in the family lace-making business, and the spiritual fruitfulness of their lives, personally and through their children, are well documented. A few examples will manifest this concretely.

Writing of Louis and Zélie, their daughter Céline recalls:

At Alençon, I was present on several occasions when my mother shared with him the honor and merit of good works. I remember a poor tramp whom they found worn out by the roadside. They brought him to our house, gave him plenty of nourishing food, then got better clothes and boots for him. While he was trying these on, his face beamed with such a happy look that after all these years—I was then only about seven years old—the scene is still vivid to me. Finally, he was invited to come back to us whenever he was in need again. In the meanwhile, on inquiry Father found out that this poor man, all alone in the world, used to lodge in a barn and beg his bread at the entrance of the military barracks. After several attempts and formalities, my father succeeded in having him accepted by the Little Sisters of the Poor.[72]

Céline speaks of Zélie's care for those the family employed, "treating them with consideration." Zélie "visited their homes and saw to it that they needed nothing."[73]

Of Louis, Céline attests:

If on his way through the streets he met an intoxicated man, he gave the man his arm and helped him home, accompanying his charitable act with a good remonstrance. Once he came across a drunken workman, who had fallen into the stream. When he helped the man up, he himself carried the toolbox, and led the man home. Another time having seen in the railway station a poor epileptic who had not enough money for his fare, Father took off his hat, placed an offering in it, and went round to all the other passengers begging for him. Then after collecting the price for the journey, he settled the man in the railway carriage himself.[74]

Céline describes a further experience:

A little incident comes to my mind. My father's teeth were perfect, and I saw him go to a dentist only once for an extraction. In spite of all the dentist's efforts, he could not

---

[72] Martin, *The Father of the Little Flower*, 20.
[73] Ibid., 23.
[74] Ibid.

even move the tooth. Father, realizing that the dentist was disturbed about his professional reputation, if this should become known, then kindly said: "I shall not mention it to a soul!" and he kept his word.[75]

With regard to Zélie:

One day while travelling, she reproved another lady in the railway carriage who showed displeasure at the arrival of a poor woman with her two babies. When they reached Alençon, mother helped the woman with her children and parcels to get to her home. Father, who had been waiting at the station, also helped; and it was midnight before they reached their own home.[76]

During Thérèse's cause of canonization, their oldest daughter, Marie, testified:

Our parents had the reputation of being extraordinarily devout. Mother observed Lent without availing herself of any lawful mitigations [of the forty days of fasting], and both of them attended 5:30 Mass every morning, because, they said, it was the poor people's Mass. They received Communion frequently, more than once a week, which was rather exceptional at that time. At Lisieux, my father received Communion four or five times a week.... Mother was very energetic and lively, but without any harshness, and she had a very sensitive and generous heart. Above all, she had the spirit of self-denial, which made her forgetful of herself, and she worked with great fortitude so as to have the means of giving us a good Christian upbringing. In sorrow, too, for

[75] Ibid., 25.
[76] Martin, *The Mother of the Little* Flower, 69.

example at the death of my brothers and sisters, she showed wonderful strength of soul. One could see from her letters that she was brokenhearted, but her faith helped her to rise above it all.[77]

The Mass ... and raising children. The Mass ... and daily work at home and in business. The Mass ... and concern for a man in need. The Mass ... and assistance to a struggling mother. The Mass ... and care for a dentist's reputation. The Mass ... and a man who was ill. The Mass ... and the courage to bear sorrow in the family. The Mass as our encounter with Jesus's word, as the reception of his Body and Blood ... and our daily lives.

The Mass is about to conclude, and we prepare to return to our activities. Venerable Bruno writes, "At the words 'Go forth, the Mass is ended,' I will seek the sentiments and the heart of an apostle."

Venerable Bruno cites these words in Latin, "At the words *Ite missa est*."[78] The Mass takes its title from the word *missa*, a form of the verb "to send." Venerable Bruno is deeply conscious that when we rise, genuflect, walk down the aisle, leave the church, and head to the street or to our cars, these are not simply physical actions. We do this because *we are sent: Ite* [Go], *missa est* [you are sent].[79] Jesus sends us from the table of his Word and his Body, from the Mass, to the world of our daily lives. As Mass ends, we can hear in a special way Jesus's words, "As the Father has sent me, so I send you" (John 20:21).

---

[77] Quoted in Christopher O'Mahoney OCD, ed., *St. Thérèse by Those Who Knew Her: Testimonies from the Process of Beatification* (Dublin: Veritas Publications, 1995), 84–85.

[78] Venerable Bruno abbreviates this: "At the *Ite* [*missa est*]."

[79] Literally, "It is sent," with the meaning given here.

He sends us, Venerable Bruno writes, as *apostles*. The word "apostle" means exactly this, "one who is sent." Venerable Bruno sees in Acts 15:26 the portrait of an apostle: Paul and Barnabas are men "who have dedicated their lives to the name of our Lord Jesus Christ."[80] We are apostles when, in our vocations as husbands and wives, parents and children, brothers and sisters, in our various professions in the world, and in our life in the Church, we have *dedicated our lives to the name of our Lord Jesus Christ*. When the words "Go forth, the Mass is ended" are proclaimed, we receive the call to exit the church and reenter the world in this way, as apostles. In a very real sense, the end of the Mass is a beginning.

Venerable Bruno invited us to enter the church for Mass with the sentiments and heart of Simeon, joyfully conscious that he will encounter Christ. Bruno now calls us to depart from the church with the sentiments and heart of an apostle, aware that Jesus sends us into our world.

Each time we leave church after Mass, we can hear anew, and in the specific circumstances of the day that lies ahead—time with our families, engagement with work, rest, interactions with others, and all that fills the day—his great commission to his disciples: "Go, therefore, and make disciples of all nations" (see image 10). We can also hear his accompanying promise, "And behold, I am with you always, until the end of the age" (Matt. 28:19, 20).

The rite of Mass provides various formulations of this sending. Take a moment now and reflect briefly on each:

Go forth, the Mass is ended: Go forth from this church now: the Mass is complete. You have been nourished at the

---

[80] *Un'esperienza*, 149.

A Biblical Way of Praying the Mass

table of the Word and of the Body of Christ. Now *go forth* and bring this richness to those you encounter.

Go and announce the Gospel of the Lord: By the way you live, by the way you interact with others, by the holiness of your life, and by your words, *announce the Gospel of Jesus.*

Go in peace, glorifying the Lord by your life: As you exit the church, let the peace of Jesus fill your heart. Seek now to *give glory to God*—that is, to make Jesus known and loved by the way you live.

Ask for the grace to leave Mass and return to your activity in this way.

17

Eucharistic Fire

I will go forth from the altar as if breathing fire.

—Venerable Bruno Lanteri

Eucharistic fire. Venerable Bruno seeks to depart from Mass with a heart enkindled, warmed, set aflame by his encounter with Jesus in the Mass. What stirrings fill your heart after our review of his approach to the Mass? What sentiments? What desires? What requests to the Lord? Might it help to pause here and share these with the Lord?

I have always loved the simplicity of Venerable Bruno's method, its ease, and its emphasis on the heart. Understanding of the Mass undergirds it, but his focus is the heart. Venerable Bruno does not present complex thoughts, each to be pondered in depth; rather, he proposes a single glance of the heart as the way to *pray* the successive parts of the Mass. The "sentiments and heart" of each biblical figure lead to the core of the respective part of the Mass. The approach is warm, inviting, alive. Because it is biblical, it is timeless.

I appreciate the way Venerable Bruno limits this approach. The Mass comprises many elements: dialogues between priest and

A Biblical Way of Praying the Mass

people, prayers of varying lengths, hymns, rites, readings, gestures. Within this multiplicity, Venerable Bruno focuses on what is central. He does not overwhelm us. The heart can keep pace.

The radius of the sentiments and heart of each biblical figure tends to expand over time. For years, I thought of the tax collector's heart as I prayed the "I confess to almighty God." Now that attitude of heart—at least when I am attentive!—includes the "Lord, have mercy" as well. This is unplanned. It simply happens as time passes, and I continue to apply this method.

Increasingly, therefore, the look of the heart unifies the parts of the Mass. The Penitential Rite, for example, consists of multiple elements: an initial invitation ("Brothers and sisters, let us acknowledge ..."); a pause of silence for self-examination; a prayer in common ("I confess to almighty God ..."); the priest's response ("May almighty God have mercy on us ..."); and the threefold prayer for mercy ("Lord, have mercy ... Christ, have mercy ... Lord, have mercy ..."). When I pray all of these with "the sentiments and the heart of the tax collector," they join in a single prayer for mercy. Again, hearing the readings from the Old and New Testaments—these may present a variety of biblical settings and themes—with "the sentiments and heart of a disciple" unifies the Liturgy of the Word. The same may be said for other parts of the Mass.

When I pray the Mass with Venerable Bruno's approach, on some days one or another of the biblical figures may come to the fore. On one day, for example, I may find myself especially aware of the heart of a disciple as the readings are proclaimed. On another, I may be alive to the attitude of a *mendico* as I pray the Our Father. On these days, the other biblical figures may be present but with less emphasis. None of this is planned or forced. I find that, as the days pass with their varying emphases, the whole of Venerable Bruno's approach tends to appear.

I find that what is true of prayer in general applies also to Venerable Bruno's approach to the Mass. On some days, I experience his approach as alive and uplifting. I am grateful for the way it helps me pray the Mass. On others, perhaps when I am tired, anxious, or distracted, I experience the various sentiments less. I understand this as normal in the spiritual life. The key, I believe, is to persevere without being surprised or ashamed, and without losing heart.

As mentioned earlier, I have taped a copy of Venerable Bruno's text on the wall near where I celebrate Mass. It reminds me of his approach every time I celebrate Mass. The summary provided in the next section of this book may serve a similar purpose.

Growth in this way of praying the Mass occurs gradually as we apply it over the months and years. Venerable Bruno composed it for himself as a seminarian and practiced it through the forty-nine years of his priesthood. Finding it fruitful, he shared it with the priests of his community and, through them, with us all. His approach grows in meaning for me as the years pass. Flannery O'Connor writes, "I am only slowly coming to experience things that I have all along accepted."[81] Her words apply to this practice of the Mass as well.

The more we learn about the Mass, the richer our application of Venerable Bruno's approach will be. For him, it was based on profound study and understanding of the Mass. A reading of books on the Mass or listening to digital resources will bless the application of this method.

Finally, what Venerable Bruno seeks and what we seek—that is, to pray the Mass from our hearts and with fruit—is a gift of grace. Our part, to use Saint Ignatius's word, is to *dispose* ourselves

---

[81] Flannery O'Connor, *The Habit of Being* (New York: Farrar, Straus, and Giroux, 1988), 97.

to receive this grace. Venerable Bruno's method is an effective way to do this, and the purpose of this book is to render it available. But the fruit of the method will be more God's work than our accomplishment. This awareness awakens confidence as we seek to engage our hearts in the Mass. God's love, his desire for our growth, and his promise that if we ask we will receive (Matt. 7:7) abundantly supply for our human limitations. In that spirit of hope and trust, we embark on this Eucharistic journey.

Three years before she died, Saint Thérèse wrote a letter to Madame Pottier. This woman, born Céline Maudelonde, was a cousin of Thérèse's cousins, the Guérins. She and Thérèse were the same age and had played together as children. Now, as adults, Thérèse was in Carmel. Céline was married and the mother of two children.

On this day, Thérèse wrote,

> Your letter gave me real joy. I marvel at how the Blessed Virgin is pleased to answer all your desires. Even before your marriage, she willed that the soul to whom you were to be joined form only one with you by means of an identity of feelings. What a grace for you to feel that you are so well understood, and, above all, to know your union will be everlasting, that after this life, you will still be able to love the husband who is so dear to you!
>
> They have passed away, then, for us both the blessed days of our childhood! We are now at the serious stage of life; the road we are following is different; however, the goal is the same. Both of us must have only one same purpose: to become holy in the way God has traced out for us.
>
> I feel, dear little friend, that I can speak freely to you; you understand the language of faith better than that of the

world, and the Jesus of your First Communion has remained the Master of your heart.[82]

We, too, have reached the serious stage of life. We, too, must have only one same purpose: to become holy in the vocation to which God has called us. The "Jesus of our First Communion" and of every Mass and Communion since, calls us to this. May Venerable Bruno's approach to the Mass bless our daily yes to that call.

---

[82] *Letters of St. Thérèse of Lisieux*, trans. John Clarke, OCD (Washington DC: ICS Publications, 1988), 2:865. I have translated *nous sanctifier* as "to become holy."

A Summary of the Method in Practice

When I enter the church, I will imagine that I see Simeon, who went in the Spirit to the Temple for the presentation and circumcision of Jesus, or I will imagine seeing some other fervent saint. I ponder the heart of Simeon, who hastens through the streets to the Temple, joyfully aware that he will encounter the Christ. I ask for his same sentiments as I leave home, travel, and enter the church.

In the Mass, at the Penitential Rite, I will seek the sentiments and the heart of the tax collector. I see the tax collector, humble, sincere, who opens his heart and life to the Lord's infinite mercy. I see him *set free* from sin. I ask for a heart like his.

At the Gloria, those of the Angels. I contemplate the joy with which the angels sing the praises of God's saving love and the gift of his Son. I ask for a heart ready to praise God with gladness through the words of the Gloria.

At the Prayers, those of an ambassador sent by the Church. As the priest proclaims the Collect, the Prayer over the Offerings, and

A Biblical Way of Praying the Mass

the Prayer after Communion, I ask to join with him in presenting my needs, the needs of my family, of others, of the Church, and of the world to our Father in heaven.

∞

At the Readings and Gospel, those of a disciple. As I prepare to listen, I ask to see myself at Jesus's feet with the other disciples, intent upon his words, open to their life-changing power, eager to hear his word for me today.

∞

At the Profession of Faith, those of the martyrs. I ask for the grace to say, pray, proclaim these words from my heart as the faith by which I live and for which, with his grace, I would give my life.

∞

At the Preparation of the Gifts, those of Melchizedek. When the priest prepares the offerings of Bread and Wine, I offer my own life, my joys, sorrows, tasks, burdens, hopes—all that I am and have—with Jesus to the Father.

∞

At the Preface, those of the Heavenly Court. As I hear the Preface proclaimed and pray the Holy, Holy, Holy, I think of the angels and saints before the heavenly throne and join with them in joyful praise of God.

∞

At the Consecration, those of Christ. With a quieted heart, I contemplate the love in Jesus's Heart as he offers his Body and Blood. I ask to share in his sentiments of self-giving.

∞

At the Our Father, those of one who asks for what he needs. With confidence, I express my needs to our heavenly Father.

∞

At the Lamb of God, those of one who is guilty and in need of forgiveness. With humble trust, I ask for forgiveness, mercy, and peace from Jesus, the Lamb of God.

∞

At Communion, those of one in love. Conscious of the great gift received, I welcome Jesus into my heart. Loved so immeasurably by him, I offer him my love in return. "I look at him, and he looks at me."[83]

∞

At the words "Go forth, the Mass is ended," those of an apostle. I ask for a heart ready to serve in the day that lies ahead. I ask to be his apostle, sent to bring his love and life to the people with whom I live.

∞

I will go forth from the altar as if breathing fire. I ask to be transformed by the Mass.

---

[83] Words of one of his parishioners to Saint John Vianney.

Resources

Biography of Venerable Bruno

Timothy M. Gallagher, O.M.V., *Begin Again: The Life and Spiritual Legacy of Bruno Lanteri* (New York: Crossroad, 2013)

Writings of Venerable Bruno on Hope

Timothy M. Gallagher, O.M.V., *Overcoming Spiritual Discouragement: The Wisdom and Spiritual Power of Venerable Bruno Lanteri* (Irondale, AL: EWTN, 2019)

Brief Selection of Writings

Timothy M. Gallagher, O.M.V., *The Venerable Bruno Lanteri: Spiritual Counsels for Life in the World* (Omaha: Discerning Hearts, 2016)

*Conferences on Venerable Bruno and
Overcoming Spiritual Discouragement*

https://www.frtimothygallagher.org/product-page/overcoming
-spiritual-discouragement-1

Podcasts

discerninghearts.com and the Discerning Hearts App: series entitled *Begin Again*. Sixteen half-hour podcasts. See also the podcasts on Overcoming Spiritual Discouragement.

A Biblical Way of Praying the Mass

To request prayers or share graces received through Venerable Bruno's intercession, and for information regarding his cause of canonization, go to:

https://www.omvusa.org/bruno-lanteri/

Fr. Gallagher's website

www.frtimothygallagher.org

Image Credits

1. *The Presentation in the Temple* (ca. 1430), by Álvaro Pires de Évora (Wikimedia Commons).
2. *Parable of the Pharisee and the Publican* (nineteenth century), by Gustave Doré (PP6RJC; Album / Alamy Stock Photo).
3. Nativity stained-glass image in a church in Alsemberg, Belgium (H912A4; Aurelian Images / Alamy Stock Photo).
4. *The Sermon on the Mount* (1877), by Carl Bloch (Wikimedia Commons).
5. *Triumph of Faith* (nineteenth century), by Eugene Thirion (Wikimedia Commons).
6. *The Meeting of Abraham and Melchizedek* (seventeenth century), by Peter Paul Rubens (Wikimedia Commons).
7. *The Last Judgment* (ca. 1450), by Fra Angelico (Wikimedia Commons).
8. *Christ Crucified* (ca. 1632), by Diego Velázquez (Wikimedia Commons).
9. Lamb of God stained-glass image in a church in Newchurch in Pendle, Lancashire (MC6GC2; Charles Walker Collection / Alamy Stock Photo).
10. *The Mission of the Apostles* (1861), by Jean-Hippolyte Flandrin (2AYG5A5; Peter Horree / Alamy Stock Photo).

About the Author

Father Timothy M. Gallagher, O.M.V., was ordained in 1979 as a member of the Oblates of the Virgin Mary, a religious community dedicated to giving retreats and spiritual formation according to the Spiritual Exercises of Saint Ignatius. Having obtained his doctorate in 1983 from the Gregorian University, he has taught (Saint John's Seminary, Brighton, Massachusetts; Our Lady of Grace Seminary Residence, Boston), assisted in formation work, and served two terms as provincial in his community. He is a frequent speaker on EWTN, and his digitally recorded talks are used around the world. He has written many books on Ignatian discernment and prayer and on Venerable Bruno Lanteri and the Liturgy of the Hours. He currently holds the Saint Ignatius Chair for Spiritual Formation at Saint John Vianney Theological Seminary in Denver.